# THE WESTERN RIVER STEAM-BOAT

**ED RACHAL FOUNDATION**

**NAUTICAL ARCHAEOLOGY SERIES**

in association with the

Institute of Nautical Archaeology

# THE WESTERN RIVER STEAM- BOAT

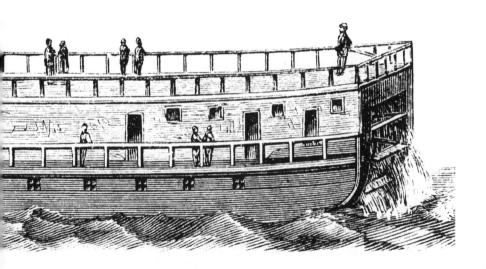

## ADAM I. KANE

*Foreword by Alan L. Bates*

Texas A&M University Press    College Station

Library of Congress Cataloging-in-Publication Data

Kane, Adam I., 1973–

The Western river steamboat / Adam I. Kane.—1st ed.

p. cm.—(Ed Rachal Foundation nautical archaeology series)

ISBN 1-58544-322-0 (cloth : alk. paper)—ISBN 1-58544-343-3
(pbk. : alk. paper)

1. River steamers—West (U.S.)  2. Excavations (Archaeology)—West (U.S.)

3. Underwater archaeology—West (U.S.)  I. Title.  II. Series.

VM461.K35 2004

623.8'2436—dc22

2003018570

*To Andréa, for her tireless support*

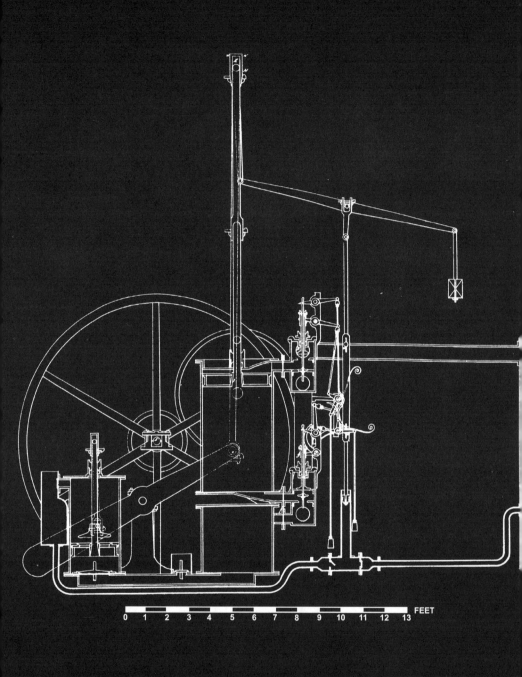

0  1  2  3  4  5  6  7  8  9  10  11  12  13    FEET

# CONTENTS

# ILLUSTRATIONS

# TABLES

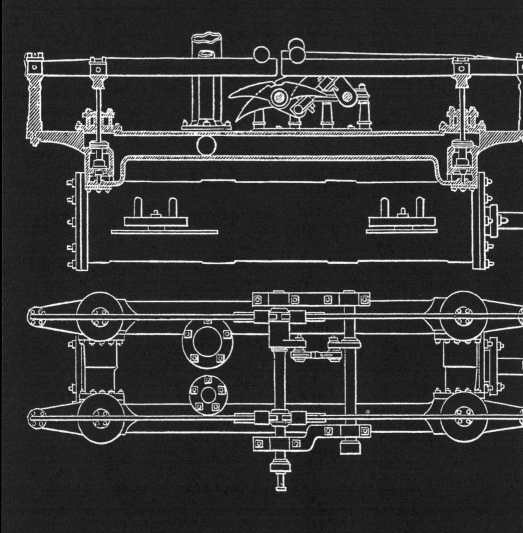

# FOREWORD

The student of western-river-steamboat history has long had access to a copious array of literature describing these unique boats after 1853. It ranges from the amusing tales by Mark Twain, known by millions around the world, to obscure deeds of sale in rural county courthouses. Information before that era is hard to find and sparing of detail. With the exceptions of Thomas Tredgold's study and the diatribes of Charles Dickens and Anthony Trollope, little was written in the popular press. *Lloyd's Steamboat Directory and Disasters on the Western Waters* gives more room for doubt than for study, dwelling as it does on the horrific and lurid catastrophes before 1856. And romantic novels such as *Steamboat Gothic* are less than useless.

There are good reasons for this disparity between eras. Prior to 1848 there was no photography as we know it today. Blueprinting was not available. The few drawings that were made were not easily reproduced and were frequently destroyed when a particular job was completed and were no longer needed. Indeed, there was not even a uniform technical language to describe the boats, their machinery, or their operations. Etchings by magazine and newspaper artists seldom show details of machinery or boat construction. Steamboat archaeology did not exist.

*The Western River Steamboat* closes many of the gaps between 1811, when the first steamboat ran on the western waters, and 1853, when the federal government began to inspect steamboats and their officers and to keep records of their proceedings. This is not to say that there was no literature about steamboats of the time. Descriptions by visitors from foreign lands, scientific papers, tax assessments, periodicals, and court records abound, but they are scattered throughout the land in dusty archives. The reader who studies the notes and sources in this book will be rewarded by the endnotes, for they will enable researchers to delve deeper into the subject than this broad outline was permitted to go. Simply knowing that these sources exist is of immense value to the student and archaeologist. Some, such as the court records of the Wheeling Bridge Case and the writings of J. M. Sweeney and E. W. Gould, are filled with intimate detail. Patent applications contain drawings and specifications.

Today, the relatively new field of steamboat archaeology is bringing forth solid, three-dimensional examples of the materials, machinery, and techniques of building utilized by the old wooden-boat builders. It is verifying and disproving the notions of what America was like at those times. It is impossible to view the results of the *Arabia* and *Bertrand* excavations without awe, for they present not only the boats but also their contents, all in common commerce at the specific dates of their sinking.

The knowledge gained spreads far beyond the rivers' banks. The briefest examination of the cargoes of these boats changes one's perspective of what mining towns were like in Montana and Idaho in the mid–nineteenth century. A society is not crude that enjoys exotic imported wines, fashionable clothing and furniture, and gourmet foods, all of which were found aboard these vessels. Machinery fragments from both wrecks clearly demonstrate that steamboats built up to 1940 had longstanding precedents for their methods, materials, and devices, many of which were found in the excavations.

Analysis of the historic mine of steamboat history that lies in and along the banks of our western rivers will be vastly expedited thanks to Adam Kane.

Alan L. Bates

# ACKNOWLEDGMENTS

This book reflects my good fortune in having the support of many individuals, institutions, and organizations in both writing the original masters thesis and in making the revisions for this book. My sincere thanks goes out to all those who generously helped me in so many ways.

I am especially indebted to Kevin Crisman for his expertise and scholarly input as the chairman of my thesis committee and for his generous sharing of information. I would like to thank the other members of my thesis committee, Charles E. Brooks and C. Wayne Smith, for their contributions of time and talent. I also appreciate the valuable insights and suggestions provided by Donny Hamilton and Frederick Hocker and the financial support provided by Texas A&M University's Nautical Archaeology Program while researching the original thesis.

While transforming the thesis into a book, I was fortunate to have the support of steamboat researcher Alan Bates. His perspective on the subject and willingness to donate his time were invaluable. I am particularly grateful for his contributing the foreword to this book.

My thanks go to the selection committee of the Studies in Nautical Archaeology Series for choosing my study to be part of the series. I am grateful too for the assistance of the staff of Texas A&M University Press.

A special note of thanks is extended to other individuals for their support and contributions to this study: Arthur B. Cohn, Lake Champlain Maritime Museum; David S. Robinson, Public Archaeology Laboratory; R. Christopher Goodwin, R. C. Goodwin and Associates; Annalies Corbin, East Carolina University; Leslie Stewart-Abernathy and Deborah Sabo, Arkansas Archaeological Survey; Steve Hoyt, Texas Historical Commission; Charles Pearson, Allen Saltus, and Renee Badon, Coastal Environments; Steve James, Panamerican Consultants; and Bill Lees, Oklahoma Historical Society.

I am also thankful for the information and leads from cultural-resource managers of the U.S. Army Corps of Engineers. First among these was Erwin Roemer of the Nashville District, but several others graciously responded to my ceaseless e-mails. Many thanks go to Thomas Birchett, Tad Britt, Mark D. Frazier, William Gaines, Michele L. Hope,

Carroll Johnson, Rob Karwedsky, Karen Krepps, Gary DeMarcay, Bradley E. Perkl, Paul Rubenstein, Kathleen Ungvarsky, Conrad Weiser, and Jim Wojtala.

Many archivists and librarians assisted me during my research. Yvonne Knight at the Howard Steamboat Museum and M'Lissa Kesterman and Sylvia Metzinger at the Public Library of Cincinnati and Hamilton County provided thoughtful support when I visited their institutions. I also appreciate the efforts of the staffs at the Library of Congress, the National Archives, the *Arabia* Steamboat Museum, the Steamboat *Bertrand* Museum, the Lilly Library at Indiana University, the Bailey-Howe Library at the University of Vermont, the American Philosophical Society, and the Sterling C. Evans and Cushing Libraries at Texas A&M University.

I am indebted to the hundreds of professional and avocational archaeologists who have spent thousands of hours documenting the remains of western river steamboats. Steamboat wrecks frequently present some of the worst diving conditions imaginable; this study would not be possible without these intrepid researchers.

I offer a sincere appreciation to my family and friends for their constant support: Walter and Lisa Kane, Peggy Kane, Nick Wyatt, Charles Kane, Ray Geremia, Jean Geremia, Gina Geremia, Dan Walker, Cory Arcak, Anthony Randolph, Sara Brigadier, Chris Sabick, Erick Tichonuk, and Pierre LaRocque. I would also like to thank June Evans of Millersville University for her many years of mentoring, encouragement, and kindness and for inspiring me to pursue archaeology. And I am deeply saddened that I cannot thank in person Erkut Arcak, a good friend who passed away much too early, for his support.

Finally, I will be forever grateful for the unwavering support of my wife, Andréa. Her patience through both the writing of the original thesis and the development of this book has been extraordinary. She also spent countless hours helping me revise and edit the text.

# INTRODUCTION

*I hardly know what to liken them to, or how to describe them. In the first place, they have no mast, cordage, tackle, rigging, or other such boat-like gear; nor have they anything in their shape at all calculated to remind one of a boat's head, stern, sides, or keel. Except that they are in the water, and display a couple of paddle-boxes, they might be intended, for anything that appears to the contrary, to perform some unknown service, high and dry, upon a mountain top. There is no visible deck, even: nothing but a long, black, ugly roof, covered with burn-out feather sparks; above which tower two iron chimneys, and a hoarse escape valve, and a glass steerage-house. Then, in order as the eye descends towards the water, are the sides, and doors, and windows of the state-rooms, jumbled as oddly together as though they formed a small street, built by the varying tastes of a dozen men: the whole is supported on beams and pillars resting on a dirty barge, but a few inches above the water's edge: and in the narrow space between this upper structure and this barge's deck, are the furnace fires and machinery, open at the sides to every wind that blows, and every storm of rain it drives along its path.*

Charles Dickens, *American Notes and Pictures from Italy*

While the appearance of such vessels may have been foreign to the likes of Charles Dickens, for most of the nineteenth century, steamboats were a part of day-to-day life for most persons living west of the Appalachian Mountains.[1] It was the thread that bound the states and territories of the Mississippi Basin together. In a thousand different ways, the steamboat affected the lives of every person in the region. Vast quantities of every commodity extracted from the western lands were shipped down the Mississippi River to markets the world over; for the upstream journey, manufactured products were packed into every available space in the hull, while on the decks above scores of immigrants and travelers saw the country's interior for the first time. The steamboat was the primary agent in transforming the trans-Appalachian West from a sparsely settled wilderness into an economically significant region of the country.[2] Its role in shaping the character of interior North America cannot be over-estimated. During the first half of the nineteenth century, the economic, geographic, and social importance of the steamboat dwarfed that of any other type of transportation. No other region of the country was nearly as dependent on steam navigation as the West, nor did any other part of the world build as many steamboats.[3]

From 1811 through 1830, the steamboats plying the nation's western waters were cumbersome and problematic machines, struggling merely to stem the river's currents, let alone carry the trade of that massive, wild region. But as shipwrights and steam-engine builders watched their boats struggle, the lessons they learned were not lost. In just a few decades, the western river steamboat was specifically adapted to the swift currents and widespread bars and shoals of the Mississippi Basin's rivers. These conditions fostered a vessel type distinguished by a shallow, flat-bottomed hull built of light timbers and braced by iron hog chains. The resulting lack of space in the hull encouraged shipwrights to construct multiple decks for passengers and cargo. The development of the steamboat's high-pressure engine complemented the structural evolution of its hull and superstructure. At all times the steamboat's development was influenced by the natural and human resources of the region. Western rivers were swift and shallow, requiring a powerful lightweight engine. With industrial centers separated by hundreds of miles of wilderness, steamboat engines needed to be simple so that repairs were infrequent but, when necessary, could largely be done by the boat's engineer. The region's vast tracts of timber and reserves of coal made the steam engine's efficiency only a minor concern. This power plant, therefore, was characteristically lightweight, powerful, easy to maintain, and immensely wasteful.

Despite the steamboat's crucial role in western development and the uniqueness of its regional design, its creation scarcely generated any technical literature, especially during the first half of the nineteenth century. The vessel's evolution was the result of trial and error by many shipwrights, engineers, and steam-engine builders. Few used scale drawings or ship's plans during the construction of steamboats. The cryptic documents preserved in the historical record provide only a partial understanding of the structural and mechanical progression of the design. Thus, this study uses data from archaeological investigations to more fully understand the physical development of the western river steamboat. While the written record may not shed light on the steamboat's structural details, these elements are not lost; they remain buried or submerged in rivers throughout the nation's interior.

This work is primarily concerned with the steamboat's development between 1811 and 1860. During these years, the steamboat was introduced to western rivers, underwent massive structural changes, and eventually reached the basic form it carried into the twentieth century. The following chapters present that evolutionary process as thoroughly as can be understood with currently available information. The existing archaeological data set on western river steamboats is far from comprehensive, representing only a small percentage of the information that, 150 years ago, was considered common knowledge to shipwrights and steam-engine builders. To date, archaeological surveys have been conducted on seventeen steamers, a shockingly small number considering the historical importance of this vessel type and the likelihood that hundreds of steamboat wrecks still exist. The quality and extensiveness of information gleaned from these wrecks vary, but it gives us the best possible look at how the vessels were built. It is hoped that future steamboat studies will substantiate and expand upon the information presented here.

This study is divided into six chapters. The first chapter presents a historical context for the technical chapters to follow. Chapter 2 outlines the archaeologically investigated western river steamboat sites. Chapters 3–5 constitute the core of the work; each section describes the structural and mechanical development of the steamboat within that timeframe. The conclusions are presented in chapter 6, followed by the notes, bibliography, and glossary. Appendix 1 contains a table quantifying steamboat construction on the western rivers between 1811 and 1880, while appendix 2 provides a table of measurements from steamboats that plied the Ohio River in 1850.

# THE WESTERN RIVER STEAM-BOAT

# WESTWARD, ONBOARD A STEAMBOAT

On July 4, 1803, Pres. Thomas Jefferson announced to the American people that their government had purchased the Louisiana Territory. Previously, the nation had spanned from the Atlantic seaboard, across the Appalachian Mountains, to the Mississippi River. This territory alone made the country one of the largest in the world, but with the stroke of a pen, a vast new expanse of land, encompassing approximately 900,000 square miles, doubled the size of the United States. Although most Americans believed in the great potential of this new region, the reality was that none of them could make an informed judgment about this terra incognita. The character of the land, its inhabitants, and even its geographic boundaries were largely unknown. Maps of the day showed large vacancies in the central portion of the continent and imaginary geographic features.

From the time colonists first arrived at the Atlantic coast of North America, they had continually pushed the boundaries of European settlement westward. This trend accelerated in the years following the American Revolution. By the turn of the nineteenth century, small farms dotted much of the territory leading up to the foot of the Appalachian Mountains, with an increasing number of intrepid backwoodsmen, trappers, and farmers cutting out an existence on the western side of this barrier. Statistics from the first census in 1790 show the number of American citizens living in the Mississippi Basin at that time did not exceed 200,000; in 1800 this number had grown to 560,000.[1] This population was small in comparison to that of the East. In 1790 not more than 5 percent of the American population lived west of the Appalachian Mountains, while the majority still lived within fifty miles of the Atlantic Ocean.

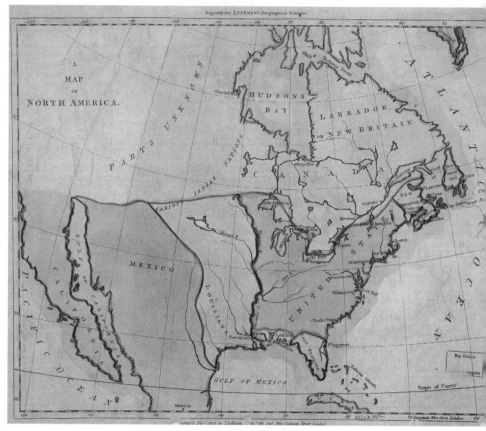

*1.1. Map of North America from 1803, showing the Louisiana Purchase.*

This geographic reality presented conflicting possibilities for the development of the Union. Jefferson envisioned a republic of farmers, a nation blessed with enough land on which generations of Americans could multiply and cultivate. It was to this end that he signed the Louisiana Purchase, with the hope that such agricultural promise would preclude the development of a country composed of extensive manufacturing capabilities and densely populated cities. The Jeffersonian view of American political economy was a reaction against the overpopulation and perceived social decline of many European countries. Industrializing Old World cities had fostered large populations of wage-earning laborers, a situation that Jeffersonians felt it imperative to avoid. This was especially important in light of the democratic nature of the American political system. Jeffersonians believed the moral decay attributed to unthinking, landless masses was at odds with the citizenry requirements of a social democracy and therefore had the potential to destroy the nation. Given these beliefs, the expansive United States could maintain its revolutionary dream only through population growth across space, thus limiting the number of dispossessed citizens and avoiding the urban degradation of society.[2]

Others doubted the ability of a democratic government to hold together such a large and diverse region, now doubled after the Louisiana Purchase.[3] A senator from Delaware, Samuel White, expressed in 1803 the potential problems associated with territorial expansion:

Our citizens will be removed to the immense distance of two or three thousand miles from the capital of the Union, where they will scarcely ever feel the rays of the general government; their affections will become alienated; they will gradually begin to view us as strangers; they will form other commercial connections, and our interests will become distinct.

These, with other causes that human wisdom may not now foresee, will in time effect a separation, and I fear our bounds will be fixed nearer to our houses than the waters of the Mississippi. We have already territory enough.[4]

The very sovereignty of the United States seemed to rest upon the question of the government's ability to bind the Republic together in the aftermath of territorial expansion. Internal commerce and the economic and social interdependence it created seemed the natural solution. Complicating if not entirely preventing internal trade, however, were the Appalachian Mountains, a fifteen-hundred-mile-long obstruction that stopped people and goods from moving freely between the developed eastern seaboard and newly colonized lands to the west. During the early federal period, many Americans acknowledged the value of improved transportation facilities, often called internal improvements, but actually building the nation's infrastructure proved problematic. The high cost and uncertain constitutionality of the federal government's involvement stalled many projects before even a shovelful of dirt was moved. The effect was that, at the close of the first decade of the nineteenth century, the East and West were directly linked by only a handful of rough roads and trails across the mountains.

Although internal improvements were not widely implemented in the West during this early period, that region was not without a means of communication and trade. Residents of the trans-Appalachian West had access to a navigable river system of unparalleled dimensions.[5] The Mississippi Basin is an immense area, roughly 1.5 million square miles, spanning the breadth of the continent between the Appalachian and the Rocky Mountains.[6] Draining this region is the Mississippi River system, composed of three major arteries: the Mississippi, the Ohio, and the Missouri Rivers. Feeding into these waterways are thousands of tributaries, ranging in scale from intermittent creeks to considerable rivers. Early settlers immediately realized the value of utilizing waterborne transportation and consequently built and adapted appropriate vehicles.

### Early Transportation

The two primary means of transportation in the West were roads and rivers. The roads across the Appalachian Mountains were the most direct routes between the regions, but by all accounts, travel over them was an expensive, arduous, and miserable endeavor. Most early roads across the mountains connecting newly established settlements consisted of scarcely more than a wide path cut through the wilderness; these were frequently in a poor state of repair. Their condition was by and large satisfactory in the summer, but during the winter and spring many deteriorated, often becoming impassable. Wagons could traverse these roads only with great difficulty, and oftentimes a large portion of merchandise had to be carried on pack horses. For settlements being established west of the Appalachians, poor roads meant that, for great lengths of time, residents were effectively cut off from the more-settled regions to the east. Early-nineteenth-century accounts of horses and wagons mired in a sea of mud are common. Writing in 1838, David Stevenson recorded his experience of traveling on a road between Pittsburgh and Erie, Pennsylvania: "Sometimes our way lay for miles through extensive marshes, which we crossed by corduroy-road, . . . at others the coach stuck fast in mud, from which it could be extricated only by the combined efforts of the coach-man and passengers; and at one place we traveled for upwards of a quarter of a mile through a forest flooded with water, which stood to the height of several feet on many of the trees, and occasionally covered the naves of the coach-wheels."[7]

*1.2. The hardships of wagon travel were well
known to nineteenth-century Americans.*

Despite the widespread desire for suitable roads, their construction
and upkeep often proved impractical and too costly in a region where
population centers were separated sometimes by hundreds of miles of
wilderness. These economic and natural conditions conspired to make
the shipment of goods overland exceedingly expensive. The only western commodities that were regularly transported to the East via roads
were cattle, hogs, and horses, which could be driven to market, and extremely valuable products such as furs, whiskey, or ginseng that could
stand the expense of the overland trek.[8]

In general, it was more economical to transport goods on rivers than
on land. Numerous types of watercraft were built to fulfill the needs of
the early Euro-American inhabitants. Light and easily transportable,
birchbark canoes were favored by explorers, while fur traders preferred
dugout canoes, also known as pirogues, because of their greater carrying capacity. Keelboats and flatboats filled the role of passenger and
trade-good carriers before the introduction of the steamboat. Both were
common on the rivers of the Mississippi Basin during the last half of the
eighteenth and first half of the nineteenth centuries and were invaluable to the settlement of the trans-Appalachian West. In the absence of
more-efficient transportation, they were essential for moving goods and
people throughout the region, but their ineffectiveness in upstream
travel hampered profitability. Without the corresponding flow of manufactured goods upstream, the flow of raw materials and agricultural
products downstream was continually hampered. Estimates for 1817

*1.3. Flatboats were simple to build and operate.*

conclude that all of the commerce from New Orleans to the rest of the Mississippi Basin was carried on twenty flatboats, averaging one hundred tons each, and 150 keelboats of approximately thirty tons apiece.[9]

Flatboats were simple vessels with boxlike hulls.[10] They were practical for transporting goods downstream, but their rectangular shape was not designed for upriver travel. "The flatboat was built on sills or gunwales of heavy timbers about six inches thick and was strengthened by sleepers. The gunwales were a foot or two high, and on top of them were mortised studs, perhaps three inches thick and four to six inches wide. At the top of these studs were fastened the rafters that were to bear the roof. The planks of the floor were about two inches thick, but the siding boards were of ordinary thickness." These craft were well-suited to the settlers' need to ship goods downstream, chiefly to New Orleans. The vessels were of such simple design that their construction required only minimal knowledge. Furthermore, construction materials were inexpensive, and navigating a flatboat took relatively little skill. Upon arrival at the final destination, the boats could be dismantled and sold as lumber, leaving the crew with a fifteen-hundred-mile-or-longer journey, generally undertaken on foot, back to their homes. Interestingly, the successful introduction of steamboats onto western rivers indirectly aided flatboating. Steamboats greatly reduced the hardships of flatboat crewmen by transporting them upriver. Moreover, the steamboat was a catalyst for river improvements, increasing the demand for waterborne commerce and facilitating larger flatboats. These factors worked to economize the labor requirements of flatboating.[11]

The other early cargo and passenger carrier on the western rivers was the keelboat. These long, narrow, rugged watercraft were designed for use on the shallow, swift rivers and streams. Keelboats were built plank-on-frame with a rockered keel and had a cabin that extended the boat's

*1.4. Poling a keelboat was a time- and labor-intensive activity.*

length. The keel was built of a heavy timber to withstand collisions with submerged logs or rocks. Steering was accomplished with a long oar that pivoted on top of the sternpost. Keelboats ranged in length from forty to eighty feet and had a breadth of seven to ten feet. Unlike flatboats, they were used for upstream as well as downstream navigation, though downstream travel was much easier. Moving a keelboat against the current was a time-consuming, labor-intensive process for its crew of thirty to forty boatmen.[12]

Given the widely varying river conditions, a number of techniques were used to stem the currents. These included sailing, bushwhacking, poling, cordelling, and warping. Most keelboats carried one or occasionally two sails, but favorable winds were sporadic at best. Often the workload fell on the shoulders of the crew. Poling, the most common method of propulsion, was achieved by several keelboat men setting their poles against the river bottom and walking along the deck's edge from bow to stern; the vessel was moved forward one boat length each time they walked end to end. Several other methods were used when the river was too deep to pole. Bushwhacking, the process of pulling the boat along by the branches of overhanging trees and bushes, seems to have been the next best option. Another technique, cordelling, entailed attaching a long rope to the mast of the keelboat, by which the crew would tow the vessel from the riverbank or along a towpath. Of course, this method was limited to areas where the riverbanks were hospitable to foot travel. The final option, warping, was used as a last resort. The crew paddled a skiff or small boat upstream and attached the cordelle to a tree or snag. A capstan or windlass in the bow of the boat was then used to draw the vessel upriver.[13]

Steamboats were introduced to the western waters in 1811, with the earliest models having little effect on the region's commerce due to their small tonnage, limited numbers, and operational difficulties. In the early 1820s the structural and mechanical characteristics of the steamboat were adapted for river conditions to the point that they were able to compete with keelboats. Although the steamboats of this era were not particularly efficient or reliable, the slow, labor-intensive process of keelboating could not compete. Keelboats soon yielded to steamboats on the routes they had previously shared, primarily the major trunk routes. On these rivers the deep-drafted steamboats encountered few obstructions and greater channel depths and were therefore more effective. Thus the keelboat was forced into the only economic niche left, plying the tributaries that steamboats could not yet service.[14] Here keelboating survived in some locations, albeit with little economic importance, into the mid-1800s.

### The Steamboat in Western Development

During the first decades of the nineteenth century, many citizens of the eastern states were engulfed in a broad societal and economic change now referred to as the market revolution.[15] This transformation shifted American agricultural society from a focus on subsistence farming to market-oriented operations. Agriculture was no longer just a labor of unending drudgery just to keep alive but now an industry that created a surplus for exchange: work now had the potential to create wealth.[16] The chief requisite for participation in this system was the availability of cost-effective transportation to take agricultural products to market.

Farmers adjacent to the eastern seaboard had advantageous access to population centers along the East Coast and in Europe, so they were well situated to join this trade. Agricultural producers in the trans-Appalachian West, however, were unable to transport the yield of their lands to such populous regions and so were little affected by the market revolution.

The consequences of this situation were reflected in the small populations of western urban centers. In 1810 the only town in the Mississippi Basin of considerable size was New Orleans. Advantageously located at the mouth of the Mississippi River, most of the West's exports and imports passed through the city's port; still, it had only 24,562 inhabitants. Pittsburgh and Lexington each had approximately 4,500 residents, and Cincinnati only 2,540. Other future commercial centers such as Louisville, Nashville, Natchez, and St. Louis were but mere villages with about 1,000 inhabitants.[17]

The absence of large markets and its effects on the region were reflected in a statement by Congressmen P. B. Porter of western New York in 1810: "The great evil, and it is a serious one indeed, under which the inhabitants of the western country labor, arises from the want of a market. There is no place where the great staple articles for the use of civilized life can be produced in greater abundance or with greater ease, and yet as respects most of the luxuries and many of the conveniences of life the people are poor. They have no vent for their produce at home, and being all agriculturists, they produce alike the same article with the same facility; and such is the present difficulty and expense of transporting their produce to an Atlantic port that little benefit is realized from that quarter." Others observed that the combination of fertile agricultural land and the lack of a market for excess produce made the pioneers indolent and lazy.[18] Farmers had no incentive to grow more food than they could consume, a task fulfilled with relative ease. Cultivating additional acreage was futile work that reaped no rewards.

Although the potential wealth to be gained by exporting western raw materials and agricultural products was apparent, the quantity and quality of these resources were immaterial without the ability to efficiently transport them to market and in turn receive reasonably priced manufactured goods. In the several decades following the American

Revolution, the essential character of the West had not changed. The region offered backwoodsmen an adventurous life and hard-pressed eastern farmers an opportunity to support a large family, but to those interested in making money, the region had little, if anything, to offer. The region's prosperity, or lack thereof, was directly linked to its inability to export agricultural products or receive manufactured goods and outside products such as coffee, sugar, and salt. The absence of efficient transportation resulted in the region's negligible contribution to the American economy. Contemporaries realized that the settlement and development of the West was dependent on its agricultural producers becoming part of an advantageous trade network. With this access and its corresponding monetary return, participants ideally would increase their production of goods for export and their consumption of manufactured articles, thus beginning a "stream of wealth, which will find its source in the increasing quantity and increased value of the products of the fertile and almost boundless west, [which] will flow a swelling tide through every channel of productive industry, trade and commerce."[19]

Steamboating was introduced to the western waters in 1811 when Robert Fulton built *New Orleans* along the banks of the Allegheny River in Pittsburgh. His initiative was followed quickly by many other entrepreneurs; at least sixty steamboats were either built or sent to the western rivers between 1811 and 1820.[20] Yet these early vessels had little influence on the region's commerce. They lacked the hull form and powerful machinery necessary to stem the currents of the western rivers, hence they could not effectively transport commodities and other goods. In the following two decades, however, steamboat construction, from the keel to the pilot house, was completely adapted to the region's peculiarities.

Many of these alterations were direct reactions to the shallow, swift waters of western rivers, but additional factors figured into this development. The region's human and natural resources influenced both the steamboat's evolution and its role in the region's development. Through much of the early nineteenth century, the low population density of the West resulted in a general lack of manpower, and skilled labor in particular was very difficult to find beyond a few isolated towns. By contrast, the natural resources of the region were seemingly endless.

Vast tracts of old-growth forest existed throughout the West, and abundant supplies of coal and iron were readily available in the upper Midwest. Given these conditions, steamboats evolved into lightly built, shallow-draft vessels propelled by powerful machinery. The building and operation of these vessels consumed vast amounts of natural resources, but the availability of prodigious tracts of timber and large coal reserves rendered efficiency a secondary consideration.

The steamboat's physical adaptation to the environment forged it into the principal tool used to settle and develop the trans-Appalachian West. For the first time in the region's history, a technology provided rapid transportation for people and goods. Not only was travel by steamboat swift, but the extensive navigable river system of the Mississippi Basin also provided a readymade network for linking the commercial centers of the West with the rest of the nation. Steam navigation brought with it the motive and means for industrialization by facilitating trade between distant population centers and providing a vehicle for transporting the region's natural resources. The steamboat's ability to affordably move trade goods provided the first stimulus toward development of the region's natural resources. No other instrument was so important in effecting the prosperity of the West.

Steam technology was not the only factor leading to this rapid economic development during the first half of the nineteenth century. Other regional and national characteristics helped create a favorable environment for the Euro-American population to participate in the national and world economies. Factors such as the nation's growing influx of immigrants, the increasing populations of the eastern states that forced many people to seek a better life in the less populated West, and the region's fertile and abundant agricultural land and large timber and coal reserves all strongly influenced the nature and course of trans-Appalachian development. These characteristics would have been inconsequential without the benefits afforded by the steamboat, which launched the region toward industrial and agricultural prominence.

The primary influence of the steamboat was its facilitation of trade. The vessels' ability to ply the western rivers provided a transportation medium by which the market economy could take hold. The increase in the region's trade and the resulting economic expansion were, however, only the initial consequences of steam navigation. A range of secondary effects stemmed from the initial stimulus. Steamboat commerce both spurred the expansion of western urban centers and increased the population density of the region as a whole. First, it provided a new means by which immigrants could travel into the Mississippi Basin, limiting the grueling overland journey that formerly was required. Second, the construction and operation of steamboats gave the region a new enterprise, requiring goods and services from a variety of other industries and employing thousands of persons.

During the 1820s, the commercial influence of the steamboat first became significant. From that point until the Civil War, steam navigation was the dominant transportation medium for the commerce of the trans-Appalachian West. Writing in 1837, James Hall accurately characterized the steamboat's role in the facilitation of trade: "[T]he imported article has fallen in a ratio equal to the increased price of western products. In looking back at the old means of transportation, we cannot conceive how the present demand and consumption could have been supplied by them." George Armroyd earlier expressed a similar line of reasoning in a more anecdotal form. He noted that, prior to the introduction of steamboats, "[n]ot a dollar was expended for wood in a space of 2000 miles, and the squatter on the banks of the Ohio, thought himself lucky if the reckless boatman would give the smallest trifle for the eggs and chickens, which formed almost the only saleable articles on a soil whose only fault is its too great fertility. Such was the case 12 years since. The Mississippi boats now make five trips within the year, and are enabled, if necessary, in that period, to afford to that trade 35,000 tons. Eight or nine days are sufficient, on the Upper Ohio, to perform the trip from Louisville to Pittsburgh and back. In short, if the steam-boat has not realized the hyperbole of the poet in 'annihilating time and space,' it has produced results scarcely surpassed by the introduction of the art of printing."[21]

The steamboat brought every product conceivable to the expanding urban centers and to the increasing number of villages and hamlets growing along the banks of the western rivers. The staples imported to the region were sugar, coffee, and molasses; these were supplemented by dozens of other products, including cotton, ceramics, buttons, hardware, fish, nails, wines and liquors, and soda ash. The goods shipped downstream differed, depending upon the port of origin, although much of the region produced staples such as hemp, corn, whiskey, flour, and livestock. Pittsburgh exported large quantities of iron and manufactured articles, such as iron implements and cookware, while Cincinnati became the nation's leader in hog production and processing. St. Louis controlled much of the trade of the Missouri River, with its principal products being pig iron and lead, animal hides and furs, and pork products.[22]

The number of steamboats and their tonnage increased rapidly after the first quarter of the nineteenth century. In 1880 the U.S. Census Bureau charted the growth of steamboat numbers and tonnage from 1811 through 1880 (see appendix 1). These data show that total steamboat tonnage and numbers grew throughout the period, although the business was greatly affected by economic fluctuations, droughts, and floods. In 1820, 15 steamboats were built with a total tonnage of 2,643, while ten years later 33 were built with an aggregate tonnage of 4,811. These numbers grew rapidly in the following decades, with 63 vessels having a total tonnage of 9,224 built in 1840, 109 steamboats of 20,911 gross tons built in 1850, and 162 steamboats with a cumulative tonnage of 32,432 constructed in the last year of the antebellum period. The growth of steamboat operations was consistent with that of most new industries, experiencing first a period of rapid growth, followed by a period of slower growth, and finally a sharp decline. The rates of growth for individual steamboats were 360 percent for 1811–20, 199 percent for 1820–30, 140 percent for 1830–40, 96 percent for 1840–50, and 38 percent for 1850–60.[23]

Steamboat productivity throughout the century was buoyed by the increasing tonnage of individual vessels due to advances in construction. The effects of these new techniques, primarily those derived from the use of hog chains and lighter timbers, can be materially seen in table 1.1. The average tonnage of steamboats increased at an even rate, while cargo capacity greatly outpaced vessel tonnage. One study of the steamboat's economic effect concludes that its productivity between 1815 and 1860 far exceeded that of any other type of transportation for a similar period during the nineteenth century. Furthermore, its success was achieved with little funding from the government when compared with canals or railroads, being primarily the result of private initiative.

TABLE 1.1. *Steamboat Tonnage and Cargo Capacity in the Antebellum Period.*

| PERIOD | AVERAGE MEASURED TONNAGE (TONS) | RATIO OF CARRYING CAPACITY TO MEASURED TONNAGE | AVERAGE CARRYING CAPACITY (TONS) |
|---|---|---|---|
| Before 1820 | 220 | 0.50 | 110 |
| 1820–29 | 290 | 0.80 | 232 |
| 1830–39 | 310 | 1.00 | 310 |
| 1840–49 | 310 | 1.60 | 496 |
| 1850–60 | 360 | 1.75 | 630 |

Source: Erick F. Haites, *Ohio and Mississippi River Transportation, 1810–1860*, p. 133.

Louis C. Hunter asserts that steamboat productivity began to decline in the latter years of the 1850s due to increasing competition from railroads. This was at first felt in passenger service and later in freight. Recent studies have shown, however, that prior to the Civil War, there was no absolute decline in steamboat operations, rather available steamboat tonnage continued to expand until the start of the war.[24]

The commercial importance of the steamboat was not limited to the trans-Appalachian West; its effect was felt nationally and internationally. The western river steamboat was one of the key links in a trade network that by the 1840s formed the backbone of the U.S. economy. During the first decades of the nineteenth century, the nature of the American economy began to change, with a decreasing reliance on international trade and a corresponding growth in domestic commerce. This change was largely based on two factors: the development of steamboats that could effectively ply the western waters and the extension of the cotton culture in the South.[25] Thus began a long period when the enterprise and capital of the country was diverted from foreign markets toward the exploitation of human and natural resources within the nation.

Cotton was the dominant export of the United States during much of the nineteenth century.[26] Its unique cultivation requirements created a circular trading pattern between the nation's three regions. At the core of the cotton economy was the labor of African American slaves. To ensure efficiency, slave labor was carefully supervised; therefore maximum returns on labor were derived from crops that required close labor organization. For this reason, agricultural regions reliant on slavery devoted themselves to the production of one or two staple crops such as cotton, sugar, tobacco, or rice. The products needed to operate slave plantations, such as manufactured goods and, to a lesser extent, food, were purchased from free-labor regions.[27]

The lack of foodstuffs and manufactured goods created an interregional trade between the North, South, and West. The South shipped its agricultural exports of cotton, tobacco, sugar, and rice to the North, foreign ports, and to a lesser extent upriver to the West. Services such as banking, insurance, brokerage, and transportation were provided to the South by the North. The North also shipped domestically and foreign-manufactured goods to the South and the West. The West produced and shipped foodstuffs to the South. During the 1830s, this pattern altered slightly as more western produce was shipped to the North using the new east-west links provided by canals and railways.[28]

Central to this trading pattern was the steamboat. The transportation of cotton was entirely dependent on the meandering rivers of the Mississippi Basin. Although cotton was a valuable product, it was bulky and difficult to haul overland. Most cotton plantations were but a few miles from the nearest steamboat landing. Here each vessel could collect hundreds and often thousands of bales of cotton. Within a matter of days, a bale of cotton would be delivered to the warehouses in New Orleans. Steamboats also delivered manufactured goods from the North and foodstuffs from the West to plantations and other areas in the South. As the trade of the West shifted toward the North during the 1830s, the steamboat was still a dominant carrier. Although these craft did not take the products of the West to their final destination, they were essential in getting goods to a railhead or to the start of a canal.

Increased commerce in the trans-Appalachian West brought with it a population surge. Not only did the steamboat facilitate the commercial development of the West, thereby encouraging settlers to migrate, but it also brought in most of these immigrants. Population increase in the trans-Appalachian West during the nineteenth century was nothing short of astounding. Nationally, the population grew from 5,306,000 in 1800 to 23,192,000 in 1850, a rate of 33 percent each decade. This far exceeded that of any other large region of the world. But the population growth of the trans-Appalachian West eclipsed even this extraordinary rate, increasing from 560,000 in 1800 to 10,520,000 only fifty

*1.5. Cotton packets transported tremendous volumes of cotton.*

years later.[29] Based on these data, the average increase per decade was 182 percent. Urban centers, particularly those along major waterways, reflected this massive growth. From 1820 to 1850, Cincinnati's population increased from 9,600 to 115,000, Louisville's from 4,000 to 43,000, St. Louis's from 4,900 to 77,000, and Pittsburgh's from 4,768 to 46,601.[30]

The steamboat was instrumental in transporting immigrants, both Americans and foreigners, to the Mississippi valley. By lessening or eliminating the long overland migration, boats eased the burden of relocating to a new region. Writing in 1888, J. L. Ringwalt described the scene on board a steamboat: "Immense numbers of passengers are carried from one part of the valley to another by these boats. Those boats which come up from New Orleans bring, besides merchants and other inhabitants or strangers, who occupy the cabin, hundreds of Germans, Irish, and other foreign emigrants of the valley of the Mississippi. On the other hand, those which descend from Pittsburgh carry hundreds of travelers and emigrants from the east, as well as from foreign lands."[31] For most immigrants, the steamboat was only one stage of a journey that encompassed several transportation mediums. An oceanic voyage prior to arrival in the West was common, as was an extended trek via wagon or stagecoach.

For persons traveling overland from the East Coast across the Appalachian Mountains, the sight of a western river steamboat was often amazing. Completing the journey overland to Pittsburgh in 1838, David Stevenson noted the city's effect upon the first-time visitor: "Here, in the very heart of the continent of North America, the appearance of a large shipping port, containing a fleet of thirty or forty steamers moored in the river, cannot fail to surprise him; and his astonishment is not a little increased if he chances to witness the arrival of one of those steamers, whose approach is announced long before it makes its appearance by the roaring of its steam, and the volumes of smoke and fire which are vomited from the funnels; but his wonder only attains its height when he is told that this same vessel has come direct from New Orleans, in the Gulf of Mexico, and that fifteen days and nights have been occupied in making this inland voyage, of no less than two thousand miles, among the meanderings of the Mississippi and Ohio."[32]

The construction and operation of steamboats spawned a number of ancillary industries important to the industrial development of the trans-Appalachian West. The growth of these industries was aided by the relative geographic isolation of the region. The Appalachian Mountains were an impediment that raised the cost of northeastern manufactured goods, thereby fostering industry in the West.[33] This trade barrier, which only a few decades earlier had hindered the trans-Appalachian West's development, was turned from a ruinous obstruction into a de facto taxation on goods from more developed areas. The initial stimulus providing a foothold for western industry was the steamboat, which fostered three supplementary industries: shipbuilding, foundry work, and lumbering.

Hall estimated that in 1832 the commerce of the western rivers gave employment to 16,900 men: 1,700 shipwrights, joiners, and laborers to build steamboats; 4,400 woodcutters; 4,800 steamboat crewmembers; and 6,000 persons employed to build and navigate flatboats. To this number must be added the persons who were not directly employed but who were engaged in ancillary fields, such as building machinery, and those involved with furnishing, supplying, loading, and discharging boats. Hall figured the total number of persons deriving an existence from western navigation to be approximately 90,000.[34] These numbers would continue to grow during the antebellum period.

Although steamboat building did not start in the West until 1811 with the construction of *New Orleans* in Pittsburgh, shipbuilding was already a well-established trade by that time. The construction of keelboats required the skill of trained shipwrights, and shipyards in Pittsburgh built several oceangoing vessels in the late eighteenth and early nineteenth centuries. The major interior shipbuilding centers throughout the nineteenth century were Pittsburgh, Cincinnati, and Louisville; however, shipyards in smaller towns, especially along the Ohio River, regularly built vessels. Wheeling, Marietta, Shousetown, Steubenville, Gallipolis, Portsmouth, Ironton, Ripley, Freedom, Beaver, and Madison all built steamboats, though no more than two or three each per year. Beyond the Ohio valley the only building center of significance was St. Louis. That city built very few vessels before 1840, but in the following decades it became the West's fourth-ranking construction center. During the years 1846, 1848, and 1850, an aggregate 437 steamboats were built in the West, compared with a total of 608 constructed in the entire nation during that time. Thus, fully two-thirds of the steamboats built in the United States during these years were built in the West.[35]

Steamboat construction was a complicated affair requiring three or four different companies. The construction of the vessel's hull and the framing of its upper works was undertaken by a shipyard. Often these shipyards were in urban centers, but it was common for hulls to be built in isolated areas and, upon completion, be floated downriver to industrial centers. Another firm then took in the hull and fitted it with steam machinery. The upper works were completed and finished out by one or more firms in charge of carpenters, joiners, gilders, glaziers, glass suppliers, sheet-metal workers, and millwrights.[36]

Steamboats required vast amounts of iron, not only for steam machinery but also for fastenings, hog chains, anchors, and capstans. The abundance of iron ore in the Ohio valley was the most significant rea-

## Western Rivers Shipbuilding

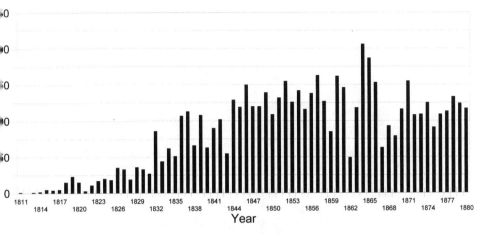

*1.6. Chart describing the number of steamboats
built on the western rivers, 1811–80.*

son for that area's prominence in building steamboats. Timber supplies
were extensive throughout the region, but the ore ensured that vessels
could be built more cheaply there than in any other location. From its
earliest days, the iron industry in the West was helped by the expense of
hauling heavy material overland from the North or up the Mississippi
River. In 1820 the cost of transporting a ton of goods from Philadelphia
to Pittsburgh was between $100 and $150. As iron foundries multiplied
and expanded along the banks of the Ohio River, especially in Pittsburgh and Cincinnati, the cost of iron rapidly dropped. In the years
1818–20, bar iron sold for $190 to $200 a ton, while in 1831, with the
creation of numerous foundries in Pittsburgh, it sold for $100 a ton. In
the 1830s the numbers of steam engines produced in Pittsburgh and
Philadelphia were about even, but by 1850 Pittsburgh had become the
nation's largest steam-engine manufacturer, primarily the result of the
demands of steamboat builders.[37]

The lumber industry, which supplied the main fuel as well as the material from which virtually all vessels were built before the Civil War, was
critical to steamboat operations. The trans-Appalachian West throughout this period had an abundant supply of timber; especially common

*1.7. A photograph of the Howard Ship Yard and Dock Company,
Jeffersonville, Indiana, showing two steamboat hulls being framed.
Behind them, another steamer is being fitted with braces for the hog chains.*

were white oak (for steamboat hulls) and white pine (for decking and
upper works). Hall states that even as late as 1850, the banks of the
Ohio River were covered by a dense hardwood forest interrupted only
by scattered towns. Wood was so inexpensive that the timber required
for vessels of comparable dimension cost twice as much in Europe as in
America.[38] Not only was timber needed for shipbuilding but also for
fuel for the engines. On the Ohio River, in proximity to large fossil-fuel
reserves, coal was burned with wood, but on most of the rivers of the
Mississippi Basin, wood was the sole fuel.

Steamboat building required immense quantities of timber. The
amount of wood used in the construction of each steamboat varied
depending on the particular shipyard and the size of the vessel. According to the 1880 census, the shipyard at Sewickley, Pennsylvania,
consumed 100,000 to 225,000 feet of oak, pine, and poplar in the construction of each steamboat hull between 180 and 260 feet long. Based
on calculations by Henry Hall, this equates to approximately twenty to

*1.8. A photograph of the Howard Ship Yard, showing the vast
amount of lumber needed for the construction of steamboats.*

fifty old-growth trees per hull. One writer in 1834 noted the economic
stimulus thus provided by this new industry: "The immense forests of
beech and other timber unfit for agricultural purposes, were, before,
not only useless, but an obstacle to the rugged farmer, who had to remove them before he could sow and reap. The steamboats, with some-
thing like magical influence, had converted them into objects of rapidly
increasing value. He no longer looks with despondence on the dense-
ness of trees, and only regrets that so many have already been given to
the flames, or cast on the bosom of the stream before him."[39]

While the construction of steamboats devoured tremendous quantities of timber, the amount of wood needed to fuel the steamers was even
more staggering. The demand for fuel fostered thousands of woodlots
along all of the navigable rivers of the Mississippi Basin, a weighty
source of revenue for residents. In 1850 the largest class of Ohio River

packets consumed between fifty and seventy-five cords of wood and 3,000–4,200 bushels of coal in a round-trip voyage of approximately one thousand miles between Pittsburgh and Cincinnati. During his travels of 1858, Charles Mackay remarked on the common sight of a woodlot: "On either bank of the Mississippi, as the traveller is borne down its steady current, he may observe at every four or five miles' distance piles of wood. These are cut . . . and heaped near the shore for the convenience of the steamers. When a steamer requires wood, it touches at any one of these points, takes what it wants, and either leaves the money or a note of what had been taken, to be settled hereafter."[40]

To expedite the process of taking on fuel, wood was frequently stored in flatboats moored to the riverbank. If a steamboat was ascending the river, it needed merely to take the flatboat in tow and transfer the wood while in motion. After being unloaded, the barge would be cast off and left to drift back to the woodlot.[41] For the downstream journey, the steamboat would tie up to the riverbank next to the woodlot while the crew and deck passengers loaded the fuel.

### Western Rivers

The rivers of the Mississippi Basin admitted steamboat navigation on up to twenty thousand miles of water.[42] The exact navigable mileage on the Mississippi River and its tributaries varied according to the season, the year, and the meandering courses of its constituent rivers. In 1848 Stephen Long calculated the aggregate extent of navigable waterways to be slightly fewer than seventeen thousand miles, although many rivers in this calculation were only sporadically traveled by steamboats of the smallest class.[43] (The details of his examination are presented in table 1.2.) Regardless of the exact figure, these rivers were unmatched in the extent of their navigability. That is not to say, however, that their attributes were ideal for steamboat commerce. To understand and appreciate the specific qualities to which the steamboat had to be adapted, one need only examine the characteristics of these rivers.

The navigable length of the Mississippi River was calculated to be approximately two thousand miles, starting at the Gulf of Mexico and ending at the Falls of St. Anthony in Minnesota. This winding riverine highway was divided into two sections: the lower Mississippi, originating at the river's junction with the Missouri River near St. Louis and running

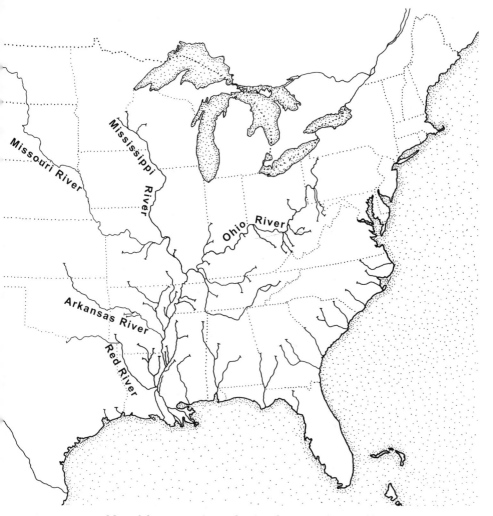

*1.9. Map of the western rivers, showing the extent of navigable waterways in the West. Based on returns of the 1890 census.*

the entire distance south to the Gulf of Mexico, and the upper Mississippi, north of the Missouri. The lower Mississippi was the trunk route for steamboat traffic; the upper Mississippi was a secondary route. The main tributaries were the Missouri, Ohio, White, Arkansas, and Red Rivers. Thousands of other tributaries, ranging from intermittent creeks to large rivers, comprised the Mississippi's drainage network.

TABLE 1.2. *Navigable River Lengths as Calculated in 1848.*

| MISSISSIPPI AND BRANCHES | NAVIGABLE MILES | MISSOURI AND BRANCHES | NAVIGABLE M |
|---|---|---|---|
| Mississippi | 2,000 | Missouri | 1,800 |
| St. Croix | 80 | Yellow Stone | 300 |
| St. Peter's | 120 | Platte | 40 |
| Chippeway | 70 | Kansas | 150 |
| Black | 60 | Osage | 275 |
| Wisconsin | 180 | Grand | 90 |
| Rock | 250 | OHIO AND BRANCHES | NAVIGABLE M |
| Iowa | 110 | Ohio Proper | 1,000 |
| Cedar | 60 | Allegheny | 200 |
| Des Moines | 250 | Monongahela | 60 |
| Illinois | 245 | Muskingum | 70 |
| Maremec | 60 | Kentucky | 62 |
| Kaskaskia | 150 | Salt | 35 |
| Big Muddy | 5 | Green | 150 |
| Obion | 60 | Barren | 30 |
| Forked Deer | 195 | Kenhawa | 65 |
| Big Hatchee | 75 | Big Sandy | 50 |
| St. Francis | 300 | Scioto | 50 |
| White | 500 | Wabash | 400 |
| Big Black | 60 | Cumberland | 400 |
| Spring | 50 | Tennessee | 720 |
| Arkansas | 600 | RED AND BRANCHES | NAVIGABLE M |
| Canadian | 60 | Red River | 1,500 |
| Neosho | 60 | Ouachita | 375 |
| Yazoo | 300 | Saline | 100 |
| Tallahatchee | 300 | Little Missouri | 50 |
| Yalabusha | 130 | Bayou De Arboune | 60 |
| Big Sunflower | 80 | Bayou Bartholomew | 150 |
| Little Sunflower | 70 | Bayou Boeuf | 150 |
| Big Black | 150 | Bayou Macon | 175 |
| Bayou de Glaze | 90 | Bayou Louis | 30 |
| Bayou Care | 140 | Tensas River | 150 |
| Bayou Rouge | 40 | Lake Bistenaw | 60 |
| Bayou La Fourche | 60 | Lake Caddo | 75 |
| Bayou Placquemine | 12 | Sulphur Fork | 100 |
| Bayou Teche | 12 | Little River | 65 |
| Bayou Sorrele | 12 | Kiamichi | 40 |
| Bayou Chien | 5 | Boggy | 40 |
| | | Bayou Pierre | 150 |
| | | Atchafalaya | 360 |

*Source:* Stephen H. Long, "Extent of Steam Navigation on the Western Waters, Including the Rivers, Bayous, &c Connected with the Mississippi by Channels Navigable for Steamers," *Journal of the Franklin Institute* 15 (May, 1848): 354–55.

Through much of its course, the lower Mississippi cut through soft alluvial sediments, as it does now, resulting in the river's tendency to meander. In this process the current at the outside of each curve is swifter
than that on the inside. With its greater velocity, the water at the outside
erodes the riverbank, while the slower water on the inside of the bend
deposits sediments.[44] This results in the river meandering into an ever
more crooked form, with the distance between two points via water normally farther than that by land. When the meandering of the riverbed
becomes too extreme, fluvial processes remove the sharp bends from
the main river channel through the formation of a cutoff, which occurs
when the river erodes through the remnant land separating two bends.
When this happens, the river is directed away from its former course,
cutting part of the riverbed off from the main channel. This former
riverbed remains as a long, narrow lake, known as an oxbow lake. Over
time, most oxbow lakes fill with sediments until they are indistinguishable from the surrounding land.

As these fluvial processes worked upon the lands, the forests lining
the banks of the lower Mississippi and its tributaries were continually
eroded into the rivers. Great volumes of timber were thereby cast into
the current. Trees and limbs floating in the river, known as driftwood,
were a constant annoyance to steamboat captains because they damaged paddlewheels and shortened the lifespan of hulls. Driftwood also
collected on bars or other obstructions in the river, and as more debris
accumulated, an islet in the river, or raft, was formed.[45] In extreme
cases, generally on the tributaries of the lower Mississippi, a stream
might become entirely blocked by a raft. These obstructions could be
many miles long, and on some rivers they delayed the progress of
steam navigation.

Although driftwood and rafts had the potential to delay steamboats
or damage their hulls, snags were a much greater danger. As a tree
floated downriver, it eventually lost many of its branches, slowly became
waterlogged, and in due time dropped to the riverbed. Frequently, the
tree's root mat, weighed down by cobbles and dirt, would sink into
the soft bottom sediments, while the remainder of the tree protruded
into the channel, thus forming a snag. Snags were divided into two
types: planters and sawyers. Planters were those that were so fixed to the

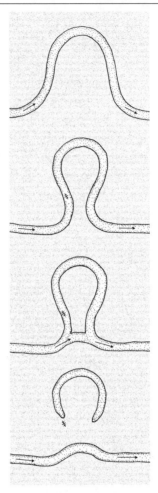

*1.10. River meanders have left many steamboat wrecks buried far from modern river channels.*

riverbed as to be immovable, while sawyers moved up and down in the current.[46] Either could puncture the hull of a steamboat, causing at best great delay and at worst the loss of the vessel.

In comparison to many of its tributaries, the lower Mississippi River was deep and presented few impediments to navigation. Although snags were a constant danger, river levels generally permitted steamboat commerce all year for the waters below Memphis, Tennessee. Above

*1.11. A sarcastic portrayal of a steamboat being snagged.*

that point, navigation was frequently suspended because of low water, often during late summer and throughout the winter. Delays were an increasingly significant problem farther north due to the smaller drainage area and harsher winters.

The navigational characteristics of the upper Mississippi River differed considerably from those farther south. The river's currents were much swifter and shallower, and thus the channel was more stable, tending not to meander. The riverbed was characterized by many rocky ledges and bars that were a hazard during periods of low water. Navigation on the upper Mississippi was at least partially obstructed at two locations. The first, known as the Lower, or Des Moines, Rapids, was a twelve-mile stretch just above Keokuk, Iowa, at which the river level dropped twenty-two feet. The second obstruction was the Upper, or Rock Island, Rapids, where the river fell twenty-one feet over fifteen miles. Both rapids delayed the economic development of the upper Mississippi valley.[47]

The Ohio River, flowing in a southwesterly direction out of Pennsylvania, forms the southern borders of Ohio, Indiana, and Illinois and the northern borders of West Virginia (then Virginia) and Kentucky. Its navigable length was approximately one thousand miles, with the main tributaries being the Allegheny, Kanawha, Muskingum, Kentucky, Cumberland, and Tennessee Rivers.

Navigation on the Ohio was greatly affected by the seasonal climatic changes of the region, with the prime seasons being fall and spring. River levels were raised in the fall by heavy seasonal rains, normally beginning in mid-September, though on occasion not arriving until December. These rains swelled the river from its summer drought level to allow navigation along its entire length. Steamboat operations were generally interrupted for four to eight weeks in the winter due to icing. The length of this delay varied from year to year based on the severity of the winter, with points farther south experiencing a shorter interruption. When the ice broke up, generally in late February, steamboats would again commence navigation. Spring river levels fluctuated unpredictably based on the thawing of winter snows in the mountains and the frequency of rains. Minor temperature changes or rainstorms might cause a freshet, a brief rise in the river, while more severe weather caused significant floods. The Ohio typically remained high until about May, gradually diminishing in depth through June, with navigation restricted to only the smallest of steamboats in July, August, and September. These navigation seasons were subject to considerable variation; rain, snow, frost, dry weather, and thaws each affected the water level.[48]

The Ohio River, for most of its length, flows through an upland area of rolling hills underlain by bedrock. Over the millennia the river cut through this terrain, and consequently its course was constrained, so it did not meander to the extent of the lower Mississippi or Missouri Rivers. Much of the Ohio is bounded by high bluffs, although these banks become less pronounced to the south.[49] Due to the stability of the river's course, it did not meander through wooded areas. This reduced the number of trees washed into the channel and hence the number of snags in the riverbed. Snags, however, were hardly absent. The semiannual flood often flushed fallen timber downstream, creating there the same consequences that befell steamboats on the lower Mississippi River, albeit to a lesser extent.

A significant impediment to commerce on the Ohio River was a series of rock ledges and rapids at Louisville. The river in the area of the falls dropped a total of 22 feet over two miles. Although their appearance was not formidable, the Falls of the Ohio made navigation on that part of the river impossible or very hazardous for about ten months of the year. Vessels that arrived at times when the river was not in flood stage would frequently have to transship their merchandise to vessels on the other side of the falls. In 1830 the Louisville and Portland Canal was opened, a major improvement to navigation on the river. The canal locks accommodated boats that were at a maximum 182 feet long and 49 feet wide. Steamboat chimneys also could not exceed 52 feet in height, measured from the surface of the water, or they would have to be hinged.[50]

The Missouri River was recognized early as the longest tributary of the Mississippi River, having its headwaters in the Rocky Mountains and eventually flowing through or forming the borders of seven states: Montana, North and South Dakota, Nebraska, Iowa, Kansas, and Missouri. Flowing into the Mississippi just north of St. Louis, the silt-laden waters of the Missouri contrast starkly with the comparatively clear waters of the upper Mississippi. The head of navigation for the Missouri, Fort Benton, Montana, is a full 3,300 miles from St. Louis, and acknowledged as the world's farthest port from ocean or sea served by regularly scheduled vessels.[51]

The conditions of the Missouri River bore many similarities to those of the lower Mississippi. Flowing through a bed of alluvial soil, it was prone to meander and became notorious for its many snags and obstructions. But the waters of the Missouri were colder, shallower, and more rapid than those of the lower Mississippi. It normally flooded once a year, usually during the summer months as snow in the higher elevations melted.[52]

The presence of a vast river system allowed the steamboat to accomplish during the first half of the nineteenth what all previous forms of transportation had failed to do. In the space of just a few decades, it helped spread Euro-American culture throughout much of the Mississippi Basin. It did this by allowing people and goods to move almost unimpeded around the region. A range of other direct effects, which were only slightly less important, also rippled through the economy. The building and operation of steamboats gave the West its industrial roots, fostering the growth of several important industries. Underlying all of this development were the West's trade arteries, the unequaled rivers of the Mississippi Basin.

# STEAMBOAT ARCHAEOLOGY

Steamboats have all but disappeared from the rivers of the Mississippi Basin, but their hulks are scattered throughout the region. The number of extant steamboat wrecks in the Mississippi valley is a matter of conjecture, but the quantity is at least in the hundreds, perhaps more than one thousand. In comparison, the universe of archaeologically investigated steamboat wrecks is minuscule. Our future understanding of steamboat machinery and hull construction will undoubtedly grow through continued archaeological study of these unique vessels.

The tendency for the rivers of the Mississippi Basin to meander has created an unusual deposition pattern for many steamboat wrecks. Over the years, as river channels have shifted, wrecks have been left in relic channels, or oxbow lakes. These lakes slowly infill with sediments, leaving the steamboat deeply buried and often far from the current river channel. Although the wrecks are no longer under the river, they are still below the water table. For this reason, the excavation of such sites has proven exceedingly difficult. After excavating enormous pits to reach the shipwreck, researchers are left with the choice of either dewatering the site or diving in zero-visibility conditions. Neither is ideal, but both options have been successfully utilized. Researchers willing to undertake such projects, however, have been rewarded with well-preserved vessels and cargos. The lack of oxygen, water movement, and light has served to encapsulate these historical treasures. Excavations have revealed that the wrecks of western river steamboats are frequently preserved up to the level of the main deck, with an archaeological wealth of cargo on the lower decks and in the hold. Those vessels buried and submerged in the nation's interior may contain the most significant and complete collection of nineteenth-century material culture in the country.

Although the archaeology of the western river steamboat is still in its infancy, the information thus far retrieved from this vessel type is significant. The following sections describe the archaeological sites from which the structural analyses in chapters 3–5 are partially derived. To date, archaeological surveys have been conducted on and about seventeen western river steamboats: Red River Wreck (ca. 1830), *Eastport* (1852), *Cremona* (1852), *Arabia* (1853), *Scotland* (1855), *Kentucky* (1856), *John Walsh* (1858), *Homer* (1859), *A. S. Ruthven* (1860), *J. D. Hinde* (1863), *Bertrand* (1864), *Black Cloud* (1864), *Ed. F. Dix* (1864), Caney Creek Wreck (ca. 1845–60), Clatterwheel Wreck (ca. 1840–80), Natchez Watercraft 3 (ca. 1879), and 3Ct243 (ca. 1883).[1] Interestingly, nine of the above-mentioned vessels have undergone investigations sponsored by the U.S. Army Corps of Engineers (USACE). More than any other organization in the country, the corps' duties in maintaining the nation's inland waterways for navigation by today's commercial vessels have brought them into contact with these relics of the country's economic past.

### Red River Wreck (*34Ch280*)

To date, the earliest western river steamboat yet located, the Red River Wreck, holds great potential for understanding steamboat construction in the 1830s. The wreckage is located in the Red River in Choctaw County, Oklahoma. The vessel was buried below a sandbank until 1990, by which time the river meandered during a flood and exposed the remains. In 1999 the Oklahoma Historical Society was informed of the site and has sponsored several preliminary archaeological studies, with the assistance of the Institute of Nautical Archaeology at Texas A&M University. Although the name of the vessel is still not clear, the construction features and machinery indicate that it dates from the late 1820s to the mid-1830s.[2]

### Cremona (*1Mb28*)

Built in 1852 at New Albany, Indiana, *Cremona* was a stern-wheeler. The remains of the vessel measured 215 feet long, with a beam of 20 feet (excluding the guards). *Cremona*'s home port was Mobile, Alabama, from

*2.1. Map showing the locations of archaeologically investigated steamboats.*

which it serviced inland cotton plantations. The vessel was scuttled during the Civil War by the Confederate Corps of Engineers to obstruct the
entrance to Mobile Bay. In 1984 the Mobile District of the USACE sponsored a cultural resources impact survey in anticipation of dredging activity in the vicinity. The survey was undertaken by the archaeological
consulting firm Espey, Huston, and Associates, during which trenches

were excavated in the bow, stern, and amidships of the wreck; the exposed areas were documented.[3]

## Eastport *(16Gr33)*

*Eastport* was a side-wheel steamer built in 1852 in New Albany, Indiana. Her enrollment lists her as 230 feet, 10 inches long; 32 feet in beam (exclusive of the guards); and having a depth of hold of 8 feet. *Eastport* was built as a cotton packet for the Tennessee River trade, running between north Alabama and Mississippi and New Orleans. In late 1861 she was purchased by the Confederacy for the purpose of converting her into an armored gunboat. While undergoing conversion on the Tennessee River, Union forces captured the vessel. She was taken to the Federal navy yard at Mound City, Illinois, where she was completed. In August, 1862, she was launched and made the flagship of the Western Gunboat Flotilla. Her career during the war was undistinguished, but the large, heavy vessel was well known for her frequent groundings and subsequent lengthy repairs. During the Red River campaign of 1864, she was damaged by a Confederate torpedo (mine) and ran hard aground near the town of Montgomery, Louisiana. Despite attempts to save her, she could not be freed, and her crew blew her up. The hulk of *Eastport* created a hazard to river navigation, and a year later the steamer *Ed. F. Dix* sank after striking the wreckage. In 1992 the Vicksburg District of the USACE attempted to locate the gunboat. The site was found using remote sensing techniques and verified by sediment core samples; the wreck lay deeply buried adjacent to the Red River. These samples indicated that both *Eastport* and *Ed. F. Dix* were likely still extant. In June, 1991, a USACE archaeological consulting firm, Coastal Environments, executed a detailed magnetometer and topographic mapping of the area, further delineating the wreckage sites. In 1995 Coastal Environments and Panamerican Consultants undertook an examination of the remains of both vessels at the request of the Vicksburg District. A thirty-foot-deep pool was dug overtop of the vessels, and the exposed structural remains were archaeologically recorded. Although diving conditions were extremely poor, researchers were able to document portions of both vessels. In June, 1995, the pool was refilled, leaving the wrecks in place.[4]

## Arabia

*Arabia*, a side-wheeler built in Brownsville, Pennsylvania, in 1853, had a length of 181 feet, a breadth of 31 feet (excluding the guards), and a depth of 5 feet, 6 inches. The boat had a short career on the Missouri River, traveling from St. Louis to points north, hitting a snag and sinking near Kansas City in 1856. The river subsequently meandered, leaving the vessel buried beneath 42 feet of sediment. Numerous unsuccessful attempts were made to locate and salvage *Arabia*, which was reputed to have been carrying a large cargo of whiskey. The wreck was eventually located by River Salvage of Independence, Missouri, in 1988. The overburden was excavated off the site and the cargo was recovered. The staggeringly large artifact collection is undergoing conservation (as of publication), and significant portions are now displayed in the *Arabia* Steamboat Museum in Kansas City, Missouri. Little information concerning the construction of the vessel has been published, although portions of the artifact collection have been studied and a book on the discovery and salvage of the vessel is in print.[5]

## Scotland *(22Lf966)*

*Scotland* was a side-wheel steamboat built in 1855 at the Howard Shipyard in Jeffersonville, Indiana. She was 230 feet long, 37 feet in beam (excluding the guards), and 7 feet deep. She ran between Nashville and New Orleans until about 1860. From the start of the Civil War through early 1862, *Scotland* transported troops and supplies for the Confederacy. In April, 1862, the vessel was taken to the Yazoo River, where it was hoped she could avoid capture and/or destruction by the Federals. In the early spring of 1863, Union forces under the command of Ulysses Grant defeated the Confederates at a number of battles as part of the Vicksburg campaign. As the Southerners retreated to Vicksburg, the defenses at Snyder's Bluff, which blocked passage up the Yazoo River, were abandoned. On May 23, 1863, in an attempt to stop the Union advance along the Yazoo, the steamboats *Scotland, R. J. Lackland, John Walsh,* and *Golden Age* were scuttled side by side to block the river; Union forces burned the vessels days later.

In 1998 the Vicksburg District of the USACE initiated a historical and archaeological survey of the Yazoo River just south of Greenwood, Mississippi. This was done in compliance with national and state historic-preservation laws prior to the initiation of flood-control construction. A remote sensing survey conducted by R. Christopher Goodwin and Associates located the wrecks of *John Walsh* and *Scotland,* which then were archaeologically documented by Panamerican Consultants.[6] This latter survey produced significant and detailed information on *Scotland.*

## Kentucky *(16Bo358)*

*Kentucky* was a side-wheel steamboat built in 1856 at Cincinnati, Ohio. The vessel had a length of 222 feet, a breadth of 32 feet (excluding the guards), and a draft of 5 feet, 6 inches. *Kentucky* saw extensive service during the Civil War and was lost to a snag in June, 1865, near Shreveport, Louisiana. In 1994, local informants reported the presence of a shipwreck near Bagley Island to the USACE. The vessel, identified as *Kentucky,* was determined to be in the path of the planned Eagle Bend revetment and would likely be affected by that construction. Over the next several years, the shipwreck underwent phase 1, 2, and 3 archaeological studies by R. Christopher Goodwin and Associates under the direction of the Vicksburg and New Orleans Districts of the USACE. In the phase 3 study, the after thirty feet of the hull was documented. Excavations revealed that the vessel was preserved up to the level of the main deck.[7]

## John Walsh *(22Lf967)*

*John Walsh* was a side-wheel steamboat built at Cincinnati in 1858. Built for the St. Louis and New Orleans trade, she was a large vessel, with a length of 275 feet a breadth of 38 feet (excluding the guards), and a depth of 8 feet. *John Walsh* ran mainly between New Orleans and St. Louis until the start of the Civil War, when she was re-enrolled at New Orleans by the Confederate States of America. She was employed in the New Orleans–Memphis trade in 1862, during which time she transported many Confederate troops and supplies. In May, 1862, she arrived at Yazoo City, Mississippi, and remained inactive at that port until the following winter. On May 23, 1863, in an attempt to stop the Union advance along the Yazoo, *John Walsh* and three other steamboats were scuttled to block the river; later that month Union forces burned the vessels. In 1998 the Vicksburg District of the USACE initiated a historical and archaeological survey that located and documented *John Walsh* and *Scotland*.[8]

## Homer *(3Ou248)*

*Homer* was a side-wheel steamboat built at Parkersburg, Virginia, in 1859. She was a small, light-draft passenger steamer built for trade between New Orleans and the Ouachita and Red Rivers. *Homer* had a length of 148 feet, a breadth (excluding the guards) of 28 feet, and a depth of 5 feet. During the Civil War, she was re-enrolled by the Confederacy and placed under contract to transport troops and supplies. Between 1861 and 1863, she actively moved men and goods up and down the Mississippi, Red, and Ouachita Rivers. On April 16, 1864, the vessel was captured by Union forces on the Ouachita River about thirty miles below Camden, Arkansas. *Homer* was brought up the river to Camden and scuttled there prior to the departure of Union troops from the town. In 1998 an archaeological consulting firm, Coastal Environments, undertook a survey of the Ouachita at the request of the Vicksburg District of the USACE. This survey located and preliminarily documented the remains of *Homer*, which were generally preserved up to the main deck.[9]

## A. S. Ruthven

*A. S. Ruthven* was a side-wheel steamboat built at Cincinnati in 1860 for service on the Trinity River in Texas. The vessel had a length of 127 feet, was 30 feet in beam, and had a depth in the hold of 4 feet, 8 inches. In 1872 or 1873, after a long career, the vessel's machinery was salvaged and the hull discarded in the Trinity River near Palestine. A preliminary investigation of the steamboat's remains was undertaken in 1997 by the Southwest Underwater Archaeological Society and the Texas Historical Commission. These organizations conducted a two-day assessment of the site, documenting as much of the wreckage as possible in the available time.[10]

## J. D. Hinde *(41Lb85)*

A stern-wheel steamboat believed to be *J. D. Hinde* was archaeologically investigated on several occasions. *J. D. Hinde*, built in 1863 at Portsmouth, Ohio, plied the bayous of southern Louisiana until 1869, when a group of merchants from Galveston, Texas, bought her. The steamboat then worked on the Trinity River until she was lost to a snag near Liberty, Texas, in November, 1869. In recent years the Galveston District of the USACE sponsored several surveys to document portions of the vessel's hull. The archaeological consulting firms Espey, Huston, and Associates and Coastal Environments undertook these surveys.[11]

## Ed. F. Dix *(16Gr33)*

*Ed. F. Dix* was a side-wheel steamer built in Madison, Indiana, in 1864. The vessel was 166 feet long, had a breadth of 35 feet (excluding the guards), and a depth of 5 feet, 6 inches. She was a shallow-draft steamer built for service on the Missouri River. In the spring of 1864, the boat began working the trade between St. Louis and points north. After less than two months of operations, she was taken out of service so that a Texas could be installed and her cabin and boiler deck lengthened. While undergoing improvements at St. Louis, disaster stuck. A fire started on board the steamboat and spread to five other vessels; losses of boats and cargo was estimated at over $500,000. A subsequent investigation revealed that Confederate sympathizers set the fire. The hull of *Ed. F. Dix* was taken to Louisville, where she was rebuilt, and she began her second career in the spring of 1865, running on the Mississippi River carrying materials and supplies for the U.S. government. In the summer of 1865, the Quartermaster Department seized the steamer to support the Texas expedition, an effort to crush Rebel holdouts in Texas. On June 23, while steaming up the Red River near Montgomery, Louisiana, *Ed. F. Dix* struck the submerged hulk of the gunboat USS *Eastport*. Although the steamer sank quickly, no lives were lost. The loss of the boat faded from memory until the early 1990s, when the Vicksburg District of the USACE located the remains of both *Ed. F. Dix* and *Eastport* (see also *Eastport* above).[12]

## Bertrand

The most informative archaeological investigation of a western river steamboat was that of *Bertrand*, located in the Desoto National Wildlife Refuge near Omaha, Nebraska. *Bertrand* was a shallow-draft sternwheeler built in 1864 at Wheeling, West Virginia. The steamer was 161 feet in length; 32 feet, 9 inches in beam (exclusive of the guards); and 5 feet, 2 inches in depth. Initially she was employed on the route from Pittsburgh and Wheeling on the Ohio River to St. Louis on the Mississippi, but with the discovery of gold in the Montana Territory, her owners decided to put her on a Missouri River run to Montana in February, 1865. A few months later, on April 1, the steamer sank after a snag punctured her hull. The engines and boilers were salvaged before the wreck was entirely lost to the river. In 1967 salvers found the vessel's remains, which by then were located far from the modern course of the river. The following year a pit was excavated down to the wreck, and, while pumping constantly to keep the groundwater at bay, approximately two million artifacts were recovered. Archaeological documentation was undertaken by the National Park Service and the Bureau of Sport Fisheries and Wildlife in conjunction with the salvers. The artifacts are displayed in the Steamboat *Bertrand* Museum, near the now submerged remains of the vessel in Nebraska.[13]

## Black Cloud

*Black Cloud,* a side-wheel steamboat built in 1864 at Orange, Texas, was used to transport cotton and assorted other goods on the Trinity River. The vessel had a length of 129 feet, a beam of 33 feet, and a 4-foot draft. The vessel was lost on the Trinity River near Liberty, Texas. The Texas Antiquities Committee and Texas A&M University undertook a site survey, which revealed the vessel remained largely intact up to the level of the main deck.[14]

## Caney Creek Wreck (41Mg32)

This vessel was a side-wheel steamboat with a preserved length of 128 feet and a beam of 24 feet (excluding the guards). The wreck lay in 12–15 feet of water in Caney Creek, a few miles south of Bay City, Texas. A team of archaeologists and volunteer divers from the Texas Historical Commission and the Southwest Underwater Archaeological Society investigated the site. They focused on recording exposed features, resulting in an overall plan view of the remains and more-detailed drawings of some of the extant machinery. An investigation of the historical record was unable to uncover the exact identity of the vessel, although the characteristics of the machinery indicate it sank after 1845.[15]

## Clatterwheel Wreck (16St182)

The well-preserved remains of a small side-wheel steamboat lay in the Pearl River near Walkiah Bluff, Mississippi. The vessel, which is generally preserved up to the level of the main deck, was documented during a single day of fieldwork by Charles Pearson and Allen Saltus. Substantial portions of the hull structure were buried, but probing revealed the steamboat to have a length of at least 84 feet, its original length estimated at 95–100 feet. The most notable features of this wreck were the still-extant port paddle wheel, pitman, cylinder timbers, and parts of the steam engine.[16]

## Natchez Watercraft 3

In 1988, during a period of low water, numerous watercraft remains were observed along the east bank of the Mississippi River near Natchez, Mississippi. In 1991, during another such period, the Vicksburg District of the USACE contracted an archaeological consulting firm, Coastal Environments, to document the exposed remains. Eighteen vessels were discovered, one of which was believed to be a steamboat. Designated Watercraft 3, it lay under a 1935 concrete-mat revetment, making its documentation extremely difficult. Information collected at the site and historical records suggest that the remains were that of *Belle Prince,* a small stern-wheeler built in Freedom, Pennsylvania, and Wheeling, West Virginia in 1879.[17]

## 3Ct243

In the summer of 1988, approximately 4.5 acres of watercraft wreckage, including two barges, a coal flat, a john boat, and a stern-wheel steamboat, were exposed during a period of low water on the Mississippi River near West Memphis, Arkansas. The State of Arkansas and the Arkansas Archeological Survey conducted a two-month data-recovery project. The remains of the steamboat were speculated to be those of *Minnetonka,* built in 1883 at Jeffersonville, Indiana. *Minnetonka* had a length of 176 feet, 5 inches; a width (over the guards) of 35 feet, 4 inches; and a depth in the hold of 5 feet, 4 inches. The wreck was broken up into several large sections, but portions were preserved quite well, including a bulkhead wall from the main deck and the chimneys.[18]

The information learned about steamboat construction from these shipwrecks has been significantly supplemented, of course, by a wealth of primary and secondary sources. In researching this topic, materials such as nineteenth-century technical journals and government documents proved very useful. A U.S. Supreme Court case from 1850, *The State of Pennsylvania v. The Wheeling and Belmont Bridge Company*, was an invaluable primary source. In this litigation, a group of men with interests in steamboating filed suit against the Wheeling and Belmont Bridge Company over its plan to build a bridge across the Ohio River, thereby obstructing navigation. Central to the plaintiffs' argument was an explanation of how steamboats were built, the circumstances leading to their unique construction, and why modifying them by lowering their chimneys was not practical. To this end, dozens of shipwrights, steam-engine builders, engineers, captains, and steamboat owners were examined and cross-examined.[19]

Numerous secondary sources were also consulted.[20] One invaluable work was Louis Hunter's well-researched and written 1949 book *Steamboats on the Western Rivers: An Economic and Technological History*, in which he delineates the structural and mechanical development of the steamboat. But he lacked any archaeological data, which since 1949 has brought to light many details unknown at that time. What follows is an attempt to build upon Hunter's foundation.

## AN UNPROMISING BEGINNING
### STEAMBOATS, 1811-20

*[I]n 1816, observing, in company with a number of gentlemen,
the long struggles of a stern-wheel boat to ascend Horse-tail ripple, . . .
it was the unanimous opinion, that "such a contrivance" might conquer
the difficulties of the Mississippi, as high as Natchez, but that we of the
Ohio must wait for some more happy "century of inventions."*
George Armroyd, *A Connected View of the
Whole Internal Navigation of the United States*

When steam navigation was introduced to the western rivers in 1811, it
was an unrefined science; the extensive process of trial and error, design
and redesign, had just begun. There was little uniformity in hull construction, superstructure, or machinery among these early steamboats.
This variety was also caused by the widespread origins of vessels and
machinery: some steamboats were built on the East Coast and imported
to the West, some had machinery of eastern manufacture installed
on hulls built in the West, and others were built entirely in the West.
For these reasons the examination of this early stage of steamboat
development is difficult. The lack of common characteristics between
vessels makes any attempt at generalization difficult. Our understanding of this period may eventually be aided by archaeological studies
(though as of publication, no remains from these early steamboats have
been located).

An analysis is best accomplished by examining individual early steamboats to which mechanical or structural innovations can be attributed.
The discussion of these craft will underscore the range of designs during
this period. The reader will note that this is not a strict progression of all
the earliest steamboats, rather it is a discussion of key individual vessels.

Steamboats were introduced to the western rivers in 1811, when Nicholas Roosevelt, under the direction of Robert Fulton and Robert Livingston, built *New Orleans*. They chose Pittsburgh, a city already established as the industrial center of the trans-Appalachian West, in which to embark on this experiment. Even with Pittsburgh's growing industrial infrastructure, skilled labor, namely shipwrights and machinists, had to be brought in from New York City. The keel was laid next to Beelen's Foundry on the banks of the Allegheny River, although most, if not all, of the machinery was cast or forged in New York. *New Orleans* had a length of 116 feet, a beam of 20 feet, a depth of 7 feet, and was powered by a low-pressure condensing engine with a 34-inch cylinder. The vessel was fitted with two cabins containing four berths and was equipped with two masts to augment the steam engine. The cost of its construction was approximately $38,000. Roosevelt steamed *New Orleans* from its homeport down the Ohio and Mississippi Rivers, arriving at New Orleans in January, 1812. After this initial voyage she was employed in the New Orleans–Natchez trade because the shallow waters above Natchez prevented her from ascending beyond that point. She was wrecked on a snag in 1814.[1] Figure 3.1 shows a contemporary drawing of Fulton's steamboat *Paragon*, built on the Hudson River the same year *New Orleans* was built on the Allegheny. Although *Paragon* was a larger vessel, the steamboats had many similarities, such as below-deck cabins, auxiliary sails, diminutive paddle wheels, and low-pressure condensing engines.

Before building *New Orleans*, Fulton had established himself as America's leading steamboat builder and promoter of steam navigation. In 1807 he oversaw the construction of *North River Steamboat*. Although not the country's first steam-powered vessel, it is widely acknowledged as the first commercially successful one. Fulton built his first steamboats on the waters of the Hudson River. But he understood that in the coming years steam navigation on the western rivers would be economically more important and profitable than on the less extensive eastern rivers. To this end, he built his early steamboats with flat bottoms and vertical sides, under the presumption that this hull form would best suit the shallow waters of the West. Interestingly, after some experience with this hull type, he was apparently dissatisfied with its

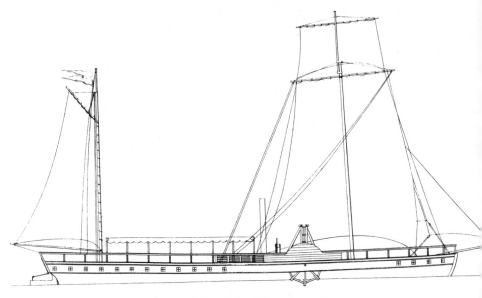

3.1. *Robert Fulton's* Paragon, *1811.*

characteristics, for his later steamboats had rounded hulls. *New Orleans's* hull was built like that of an ocean-going ship, despite its intended use in shallow waters.[2]

During the early development of steam technology, monopolies granting exclusive steam-navigation rights were routinely awarded by the states to entrepreneurs. The intent was to encourage experimentation in this new and untested field by guaranteeing profits, to the extent possible, if the venture succeeded. Fulton and Livingston had previously received such rights on the waters of New York State and attempted the same in the trans-Appalachian West, petitioning the legislatures of Ohio, Kentucky, Tennessee, and the Upper Louisiana Territory.[3] Their requests were largely rejected, with the exception of Louisiana. There they were granted exclusive privileges, much to the irritation of residents in areas to the north. The northern states and territories viewed this act as adversely affecting the navigation of the entire Mississippi Basin since Louisiana contained the port of New Orleans, the entrepôt that collected nearly all of the region's trade. Restrictions at this key city could have been detrimental to all upriver areas, but other entrepreneurs ignored the law, and thus many steamers plied the waterways of Louisiana in violation of the monopoly. The Fulton-Livingston agreement was officially lifted in 1824 with the Supreme Court case *Gibbons v. Ogden.*

The second steamboat on western waters was the diminutive stern-wheeler *Comet,* built in 1813. *Comet* had a length of 52 feet, a beam of 8 feet, and was twenty-five tons burden. This vessel was built in Brownsville, Pennsylvania, with an engine based on a patent granted to Daniel French in 1809 for an oscillating, high-pressure steam engine for propelling boats. This was the first use of a high-pressure engine on the western rivers. The patent drawing of French's oscillating engine reveals much about the construction of the engine and the hull it was placed in. It clearly shows an efficient design, especially in the means of transferring the force of the piston to the paddle wheel. The cylinder oscillated on trunnions as the piston moved back and forth and the paddle-wheel crank rotated. Unlike the Boulton and Watt engines that Fulton favored, French's engine avoided awkward gearing and inefficient transmission of power. The patent drawing also shows an important construction feature: the placement of the paddle wheel inside the lines

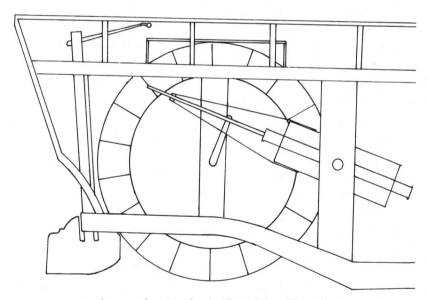

*3.2. A patent drawing showing Daniel French's oscillating
cylinder transmitting its power to a stern wheel.*

of the hull. For the earliest stern-wheelers, this location was typical, almost certainly because placing the paddle wheel aft of the hull caused too much hull distortion. (Stern wheels extending aft of the hull would not be feasible until the advent of hog chains in the late 1830s.) Despite *Comet*'s innovative machinery, the vessel does not seem to have functioned well. It made several journeys between Natchez and New Orleans, ignoring the Fulton-Livingston monopoly, but after less than one year of service, the engine was removed and sold to either a cotton gin or a sawmill.[4]

The third steamboat on the western waters was Fulton's *Vesuvius*. Built in 1814 at Pittsburgh, it had a length of 160 feet, a beam of 30 feet, and drew 6 feet of water loaded. The vessel was powered by a low-pressure condensing engine of unknown origin.[5] A square sail in the bow augmented the steam power plant. The machinery was placed in the hold about amidships, while the area abaft was used for cargo. Passenger quarters were located in a quarter deck 8 feet high and 60 feet in length. Above the quarterdeck was a promenade shaded by a canopy. Fortunately, an excellent firsthand account of *Vesuvius* exists, penned by Edouard de Montulé, who traveled on the vessel in 1816 or 1817.

Although not explicitly stated, Montulé's description reveals *Vesuvius* was propelled by a low-pressure engine. He notes that the boat had a large boiler in which the steam was raised and from there forced into a cast-iron pipe. The pipe divided into two branches, one going into the top of the cylinder and the other into the bottom. The heavy iron piston was moved inside the cylinder as steam was either let in or exhausted from the top or bottom of the cylinder.[6]

The most telling part of Montulé's description is what he does not mention, namely a condenser. Fulton built all of his steamboats on the low-pressure-condensing-engine plan pioneered by Boulton and Watt, yet Montulé's description is more akin to a high-pressure noncondensing engine. He goes on to write of the dangerous pressure of steam in the boiler and a safety valve that carried a weight of sixteen pounds. His account provides the first indication that low-pressure condensing engines were not well suited to the western rivers. It seems that *Vesuvius*'s engineer had disconnected the condenser and was exhausting the steam directly into the air. He likely did this because high-pressure

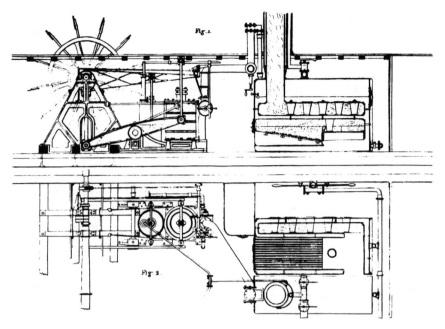

*3.3. The profile view and plan of the low-pressure condensing engine used by Robert Fulton in his early steamboats.*

steam imparted more power to the paddle wheel, giving the relatively weak power plant more force to counter the river currents. Disconnecting the condenser would also eliminate the detrimental accumulation of sediment in that part, a common problem when making steam from silt-laden river water.[7] Montulé unwittingly offers a glimpse at a brief period when a low-pressure condensing engine was being made to work like a high-pressure engine.

*Enterprise* was Daniel French's second steamboat and the fourth on western rivers. Apparently, French was able to overcome some of the technical difficulties he had run into with *Comet,* for *Enterprise* seems to have run more successfully. The forty-five-ton vessel had a length of 60–70 feet, a beam of 15 feet, and drew approximately 2½ feet of water.[8] Following his patent, the engine was a twenty-four-horsepower, oscillating high-pressure engine. Steam was raised in two cylindrical boilers 25 feet long and 27 inches in diameter with at least one flue through each.[9]

*Enterprise* had several successful voyages under Capt. Henry Shreve and was credited as being the first steamboat to make the upriver journey from New Orleans to Louisville and then on to Pittsburgh.[10]

*Washington,* a four-hundred-ton stern-wheeler built by Henry Shreve in Brownsville, Pennsylvania, is typically viewed as the prototype of the later western river steamboats because of its engine type and layout.[11] The diary of William Mercer, who traveled on the vessel in 1816, is the most complete, contemporary account of the vessel's structure and machinery.

The boiler is placed midships on the deck, and is heated by a furnace placed at either end. The steam is conveyed through two tubes to the machinery, which is under deck in the after part of the boat, and which, being set in motion, turns a single water wheel, placed near the stern, and concealed from the view of persons on the deck by a gentle elevation of the flooring timber. The arrangement below, is also, different. A common cabin about 80 feet long extends from the centre to either end. In the stern it opens into two apartments, one of which is a drawing room, and the other a dormitory, both appropriated, exclusively, to the use of the ladies. Towards the bow there are, also, two rooms, one of which is the private apartment of the captain and in the other, the bar is kept. In the large, common room, there are 20 berths, above & below, on either side of which is calculated for the accommodation of two lodgers.[12]

Much of the historical evidence regarding *Washington* is contradictory, although it does appear that Shreve was the first person to employ a horizontally oriented high-pressure engine. This attribute, as well as the placement of the boilers on the main deck, was adopted on nearly all later western river steamboats. The engine had a six-foot stroke and a cylinder with a diameter of twenty-four inches. It had a powerful one-hundred-horsepower engine that weighed only 9,921 pounds. The 1816 loss of *Washington* and seven of its passengers when one of its boilers burst was the first of many explosions on the western rivers.[13]

*General Pike,* a stern-wheeler built in 1818 at Cincinnati, was the first steamboat built exclusively for the conveyance of passengers. Accordingly, her accommodations were spacious, and she was superbly furnished. This vessel, powered by a high-pressure engine, was 100 feet on the keel, had a breadth of 25 feet, and drew only 39 inches of water.

*3.4. Profile of the stern-wheeler* General Pike.

*3.5. Profile of* Maid of Orleans.

*General Pike*'s cabin was 40 feet in length and composed of fourteen staterooms and a saloon that ran the cabin's length. The vessel was equipped to carry one hundred passengers.[14] *General Pike*'s stern wheel was mounted inside the lines of the hull, which was intended to protect it from driftwood.

*Maid of Orleans* was an eastern-built steamboat that found its way to the western rivers. This 193-ton vessel was built in 1818 at Philadelphia and sailed from that port to New Orleans for use on the Mississippi River. The depiction of the craft shows it had a walking-beam engine,

*3.6. A depiction of Stephen Long's* Western Engineer.

bowsprit, transom stern, and cabins below the main deck. The vessel was originally equipped with two masts and was rigged as a schooner, but the masts were removed sometime after its arrival in the West. It was propelled by a low-pressure condensing engine with a copper boiler, which exploded on the Savannah River, killing six persons. The *Maid of Orleans*'s loss in Georgia confirms Gould's assertion that she was built for both river and sea navigation.[15]

One of the most unique early steamboats was *Western Engineer,* built at Pittsburgh in 1818 under the supervision of Maj. Stephen Long of the U.S. Topographical Engineers. A stern-wheeler with a length of 75 feet and a breadth of 13 feet, *Western Engineer* was designed for an expedition up the shallow Missouri River, and consequently the hull drew only 30 inches of water. Its most unusual feature was the serpentine fig-urehead from whose mouth spent steam was vented, an apparent at-tempt to gain the respect of and/or instill fear in the Native Americans it might encounter. The high-pressure engine had one improvement that was subsequently incorporated on all later western river steam-boats. "By . . . use of the cut off cam . . . , the steam is made to act with its full (or boiler) force through about five-eights of every stroke of the piston; and by its inherent or expansive force only, through the residue of the stroke, thus nearly doubling the efficiency of the steam power, in comparison with that previously employed in western river boats." *West-ern Engineer* was powered by three cylindrical boilers 15 feet long and 20 inches in diameter. They carried a working pressure of 96 pounds per square inch, which was raised on occasion to 128 pounds.[16]

Although *Western Engineer* may have been designed for steaming on the shallow waters of the Missouri River, it had little in common with the mountain boats that would eventually make that run with regularity. One depiction shows the stern wheel clearly recessed into the lines of the hull. The machinery, both boilers and engines, are located below the deck.[17] The sketch also indicates that there were cabins below deck and that a covered quarterdeck extended along the aft third of the ves-sel. The steamboat was also equipped with a mast and sail, a necessity given how far it was traveling from repair facilities.

*Structure*

The earliest steamboats on the western rivers bore little resemblance to the midcentury western river steamboat. During this time, shipwrights experimented with hull form, cabin arrangement, and paddle-wheel structure and placement. Adapting steamboats to western rivers was a process of trial and error in which the lack of an accepted way of build-ing them meant that there was no consensus on their ideal form.

In general, steamboats of this period were characterized by heavily built deep-draft hulls with a marked sheer. Hull form was more consis-tent with ocean-going vessels than with craft expected to travel on shal-low rivers, although some modifications based on river conditions were implemented with surprising rapidity. Hulls were constructed with double frames and thick planking to protect against impacts with snags, drift wood, and ice. Additionally, many early steamboats were equipped with a snag chamber.[18] This transversely oriented, watertight bulkhead was designed to prevent the entire hull from flooding when a snag punctured the bow. Many steamboats were still equipped with sails for harnessing wind power when necessary. Other features such as figureheads and bowsprits were also common during this period, but all of these would be discarded in the coming decades.[19] The deep hulls of early steamboats provided enough room in the hold to transport both cargo and passengers. Passenger's quarters were commonly located below decks, though some steamboats did have a cabin that spanned the after section of the main deck. Either of these two types would often have a section of the uppermost deck covered by an awning so that passengers could be outside but protected from the elements.

Many of the early steamboats were quite small since the earliest shipwrights addressed the shallow-draft problem by building smaller vessels, which naturally drew less water.[20] Table 3.1 quantifies the steamboats built during this period and reflects this trend. The lowest vessel tonnage is 15, while the largest is 644. For the ninety-two steamboats that have tonnage information, the average tonnage is 187.5 and the median tonnage is 150. Building these smaller steamboats not only limited the vessel's draft but also constrained cargo capacity.

As future archaeological surveys locate some of these early steamboats, their hull forms will almost certainly show us that they can be broken down into two types: flat bottomed and round bottomed. Although Robert Fulton was an early advocate of flat-bottomed hulls for steamboats, it appears that he was dissatisfied with that style and built all of his western boats with round hulls. The reasoning behind this modification is unclear. It seems certain, however, that most of these early steamboats, especially those that were built in the West (the overwhelming majority), had flat-bottomed hulls. Their forms, however, would not bear much resemblance to the flat-bottomed hulls of the western river steamboats of the 1840s. None of these early hulls were braced by hog chains, thus they would need to be staunchly built in order to support the weight of machinery and cargo. The most interesting hull forms of the day certainly belonged to the stern-wheelers. Unlike later versions, these early boats had the paddle wheel housed within a watertight trunk

LE 3.1. *Steamboats Built for Western Rivers, 1811–20.*

| ES | TYPE OF ENGINE | WHERE BUILT | WHEN BUILT | TONNAGE | DATE OF LOSS | HOW DESTROYED |
|---|---|---|---|---|---|---|
| a | | Pittsburgh | 1814 | 361 | 1822 | Worn out |
| ama | | Fort Stephens | 1818 | 219 | 1824 | Struck *S. B. Natchez* |
| ndria | | New Orleans | 1819 | 60 | 1823 | Struck a drift log |
| heny | High pressure | Pittsburgh | 1818 | 50 | 1826 | Worn out |
| e Packet | | Pittsburgh | 1819 | 50 | | |
| loe | | Pittsburgh | 1816 | 250 | 1819 | Worn out |
| un | High pressure | Kentucky River | 1819 | 130 | 1824 | Worn out |
| f Commerce | High pressure | Pittsburgh | 1819 | 221 | 1822 | Worn out |
| nnati | | Cincinnati | 1818 | 157 | | Snagged |
| nbus | Low pressure | New Orleans | 1819 | 450 | 1824 | Worn out |
| et | High pressure | Cincinnati | 1817 | 154 | 1823 | Snagged |
| ier | Low pressure | Louisville | 1820 | 119 | | Worn out |
| berland | High pressure | Pittsburgh | 1819 | 246 | 1825 | Worn out |
| atch | | Brownsville | 1817 | 75 | 1820 | Worn out |
| hin | High pressure | Pittsburgh | 1819 | 146 | 1834 | Worn out |
| e | | Cincinnati | 1818 | 118 | | Snagged above New Orleans |
| beth | | Louisville | 1817 | 243 | | Worn out |
| prise | | Brownsville | 1814 | 75 | 1817 | Worn out |
| ange | | Louisville | 1818 | 214 | 1824 | Worn out |
| dition | | Pittsburgh | 1818 | 120 | | |
| dition | | Wheeling | 1819 | 235 | 1824 | Worn out |
| tte | High pressure | Louisville | 1819 | 314 | | Worn out |
| ana | High pressure | Philadelphia | 1820 | 408 | | Still running |
| kfort | | Kentucky River | 1818 | 250 | 1822 | Worn out |
| klin | | Pittsburgh | 1817 | 150 | 1822 | Snagged near St. Genevieve |
| Clarke | High pressure | Louisville | 1818 | 200 | 1822 | Worn out |
| Greene | Low pressure | Cincinnati | 1820 | 306 | 1823 | Snagged on the Cumberland River |
| Harrison | | Louisville | 1819 | | 1823 | Destroyed |
| Jackson | High pressure | Pittsburgh | 1817 | 150 | 1822 | Snagged on the Cumberland River |
| Pike | High pressure | Cincinnati | 1818 | 180 | 1823 | Worn out |
| Robinson | High pressure | Newport | 1819 | 238 | 1823 | Snagged near New Madrid, Mo. |
| ge Madison | High pressure | Pittsburgh | 1817 | 150 | 1822 | Worn out |
| Shelby | Low pressure | Louisville | 1819 | 106 | 1822 | Worn out |
| a | | Cincinnati | 1818 | 120 | 1823 | Worn out |
| erson | | Cincinnati | 1818 | 124 | 1823 | Worn out |

TABLE 3.1. *Continued*

| NAMES | TYPE OF ENGINE | WHERE BUILT | WHEN BUILT | TONNAGE | DATE OF LOSS | HOW DESTROYED |
|---|---|---|---|---|---|---|
| Henry Clay | Low pressure | Licking River | 1819 | 150 | 1826 | Destroyed on Mobile River |
| Hero | | Steubenville | 1819 | 120 | 1822 | Struck rock near Golconda, Ill. and sank |
| Independence | | Pittsburgh | 1818 | 50 | | |
| Independence | | Salt River | 1818 | 100 | 1821 | Worn out |
| James Monroe | High pressure | Pittsburgh | 1816 | 150 | 1821 | Sunk in the Mississippi Riv below the Red River |
| James Ross | High pressure | Pittsburgh | 1818 | 270 | 1823 | Stove by ice at St. Louis |
| Johnston | High pressure | Wheeling | 1818 | 140 | 1822 | Worn out |
| Kentucky | | Kentucky River | 1818 | 112 | 1821 | Worn out |
| Leopard | | Louisville | 1820 | 60 | 1825 | Snagged near P Chicot, Ark. |
| Louisiana | Low pressure | New Orleans | 1818 | 103 | | Worn out |
| Maid of Orleans | Low pressure | Philadelphia | 1818 | 193 | | Destroyed |
| Mandan | | Louisville | 1819 | 150 | 1825 | Snagged above Orleans |
| Manhattan | Low pressure | New York City | 1819 | 427 | 1825 | Worn out |
| Mars | High pressure | Wheeling | 1819 | 55 | 1822 | Snagged above Orleans |
| Maysville | High pressure | Maysville | 1818 | 209 | 1824 | Worn out |
| Mercury | High pressure | Steubenviille | 1819 | 15 | | Struck by S. B. Pittsburg |
| Mississippi | Low pressure | Mobile | 1819 | 380 | 1825 | Worn out |
| Missouri | High pressure | Newport | 1819 | 177 | 1826 | Snagged |
| Missouri Packet | | Louisville | 1819 | 60 | 1820 | Snagged on the Missouri River |
| Mobile | | New Orleans | 1820 | 145 | | |
| Napoleon | | Louisville | 1817 | 316 | 1822 | Worn out |
| New Orleans | | Pittsburgh | 1815 | 350 | 1818 | Sunk near Bato Rouge |
| Ohio | High pressure | New Albany | 1817 | 364 | 1819 | Worn out |
| Olive Branch | High pressure | Pittsburgh | 1819 | 313 | | Worn out |
| Orleans | | Pittsburgh | 1811 | 400 | 1813 | Snagged near Rouge |
| Osage | | Cincinnati | 1820 | 149 | 1823 | Sunk |

| ES | TYPE OF ENGINE | WHERE BUILT | WHEN BUILT | TONNAGE | DATE OF LOSS | HOW DESTROYED |
|---|---|---|---|---|---|---|
| gon | Low pressure | Cincinnati | 1819 | 355 | 1828 | Worn out |
| everance | | Cincinnati | 1818 | 50 | 1820 | Burnt near Madison (Iowa or Ill.) |
| Boy | High pressure | Louisville | 1818 | 231 | 1824 | Worn out |
| dence | Low pressure | Kentucky River | 1818 | 450 | 1824 | Snagged above New Orleans |
| de | High pressure | Pittsburgh | 1819 | 189 | 1822 | Burnt |
| man | | Louisville | 1818 | 231 | 1824 | Burnt at Mobile |
| et | | Louisville | 1820 | 75 | 1821 | Worn out |
| t Louis | High pressure | Pittsburgh | 1818 | 250 | 1821 | Burnt near New Madrid, Mo. |
| erlane | | Pittsburgh | 1818 | 307 | 1824 | Worn out |
| e | Low pressure | New Orleans | 1818 | 296 | 1825 | Burnt below Natchez |
| graph | | Louisville | 1818 | 60 | 1819 | Snagged at Island No. 21, Miss. |
| graph | | Pittsburgh | 1819 | 160 | 1820 | Burnt near Point Chicot, Ark. |
| essee | Low pressure | Cincinnati | 1819 | 416 | 1823 | Snagged above Natchez |
| nas Jefferson | High pressure | Pittsburgh | 1818 | 250 | 1822 | Worn out |
| ed States | Low pressure | Jeffersonville | 1819 | 644 | 1824 | |
| cipede | Low pressure | Louisville | 1819 | 100 | 1824 | Worn out |
| a | | Cincinnati | 1816 | 100 | 1821 | Worn out |
| vius | Low pressure | Pittsburgh | 1814 | 390 | 1821 | Burnt, 1816, and rebuilt; worn out |
| nia | High pressure | Wheeling | 1819 | 150 | 1822 | Snagged near St. Genevieve |
| ano | High pressure | New Albany | 1819 | 217 | 1822 | Worn out |
| an | High pressure | Cincinnati | 1819 | 258 | 1824 | Worn out |
| hington | High pressure | Wheeling | 1815 | 212 | 1822 | Worn out |
| Engineer | | Pittsburgh | 1819 | 30 | 1822 | Worn out |
| eling Packet | | Wheeling | 1819 | 100 | 1823 | Worn out |

inside the lines of the hull This watertight box, though, would have greatly complicated their construction and taken up a considerable amount of cargo space.

## Machinery

The steamboat engines used on the western rivers during this period can be divided into two types: low-pressure condensing and high-pressure engines. Low-pressure condensing engines utilized steam of only a few pounds greater pressure than that of the atmosphere. The driving force upon the piston was achieved by creating a partial vacuum in the condenser, which was located below the cylinder. A spray of water in the condenser rapidly cooled the steam, thereby causing a reduction in volume. This partial vacuum was created either below or above the piston, depending on its position in the stroke, which then was driven inside the cylinder by the low-pressure steam on one side and the vacuum on the other. In the early years of steam navigation, this type of engine was said to follow the Boulton and Watt plan, after its inventors James Watt and Matthew Boulton.

A high-pressure engine was worked by the force and expansive power of steam. After being generated in a boiler sufficiently strong to withstand high pressures, the steam was introduced into the cylinder either at the top or bottom, depending upon the location of the piston in its stroke. The tremendous pressure would then drive the piston. Often the supply of steam would be cut off before the piston had moved the entire length of the cylinder, after which the steam would expand in the cylinder, pushing the piston for the remainder of the stroke. At the completion of the stroke, the spent steam was exhausted from that side of the cylinder and new steam injected into the other, thereby moving the piston in the opposite direction. The simplicity of this design made it considerably lighter and smaller than low-pressure condensing engines.

# TRIAL, ERROR, AND ADAPTATION
## STEAMBOATS, 1820-35

*In the construction of the boats there has been a progressive and very
decided improvement. Their models have been changed to suit the exigencies
of the navigation. The great objects have been to obtain speed and capacity
for carrying freight, with power to stem the heavy currents of our rivers,
and the least possible draught of water. In all these respects our boats have
been improved from year to year, and are still improving.*
James Hall, *The West*

During the 1820s, steam navigation on the western rivers exited its early
experimental period and began to have significant, positive effects on
the region's economic, industrial, and agricultural life. Through trial
and error by shipwrights and steam engineers, the assortment of hull
and engine types declined by the late 1820s, and a distinct vessel designed expressly for western rivers emerged. Further modifications
in machinery, hull lines, and superstructure continued through the
century's end, but these were refinements, not revolutions. Reflecting
upon the first decades of the nineteenth century, James Hall wrote in
1846 that steam navigation had been brought from "an unpromising
beginning, through discouragement, failure, disappointment—through
peril of life, vast expenditure of money, and ruinous loss, to the most
complete and brilliant success." Furthermore, in this accomplishment
"science pointed the way, but she did no more; it was the wealth of the
Western merchant, and the skill of the Western mechanic, that wrought
out the experiment to successful issue."[1] Hall's "successful issue" was the
increasing economic efficiency of the western river steamboat due to its
physical evolution from a deep-draft ship to a shallow-draft inland craft.

During the 1820s, no place in the world had a well-established tradition of building steamboats, let alone the wilderness of the trans-

*4.1. A derisive drawing of a steamboat from the mid-1820s. Although proportionally inaccurate, the features of the cartoon vessel seem correct.*

Appalachian West. Initially, many steamboats were built in the East because of that region's industrial capability. Western rivers, however, demanded specific adaptations that could not be adequately addressed by eastern shipwrights. As such, their steamboats were imperfect in form for the West. Building upon this technological base, western shipwrights experimented widely to find the combination of characteristics to overcome the challenges of the region's waterways. Western urban centers saw more and more boatyards producing steamboats, and though into the early 1820s a few steamboats from the East were still arriving in the West, by the mid-1820s, only western shipwrights, concentrated in the cities of Cincinnati, Louisville, and Pittsburgh, were producing steamboats for the western rivers.

Geography favored western-built steamboats because their builders could observe the performance of their products and those of other shipyards. Western shipwrights were able to employ or discard design features based on their own empirical observations. Eastern builders were not witness to the results of their exported steamboats and so had little basis to make appropriate changes. Another disadvantage of eastern-built steamboats was the oceanic voyage from the shipyard to the West. A steamship designed to make such a journey would by nature not be practical on the western rivers. The deep draft and heavy construction of these vessels, so necessary for ocean conditions, were not conducive to traveling on shallow rivers. Lastly, the plentiful timber supplies of the West made ship construction less expensive than on the East Coast.[2] The cost of shipbuilding was further lowered as an increasing number of foundries were established in the major shipbuilding centers.

### Structure

Statistics indicate that between 1818 and 1835, steamboat hulls for all tonnage groups became longer, wider, and shallower. In the 100–125 tonnage class, average hull length increased by 16 percent, breadth increased by 6 percent, but depth decreased by 29 percent, with similar changes in the 200–225 and 400–500 tonnage classes.[3] The rapidity with which these changes were implemented was due partly to the disposition of western shipwrights. Theories of naval architecture and theoretical deductions based on scientific experiments had no place in

*4.2. A drawing of an Ohio River steamer from the mid-1830s.*

building western river steamboats. The evolution of this class of vessel was an incremental, yet swift, process by which western shipwrights built boats according to their own observations and sensibilities, without the use of general principles. Universally adopted rules for steamboat building were nonexistent; the prevailing rule was that of trial and error. Scale drawings were not used in the construction of steamboats of this period, and weights and displacements were rarely calculated. As evidenced by the contract for the construction of the steamboat *Yellowstone* and later records from the Howard Ship Yard and Dock Company, individual vessels were built according to the desired characteristics, including the overall dimensions and those of key structural features. Often, such a textual description was clarified only by a quickly rendered sketch.[4]

Western river steamboat development was strongly influenced by eastern shipwrights. Numerous designers in the early nineteenth century migrated from the East Coast to the boatbuilding centers of Pittsburgh, Louisville, and Cincinnati. The ocean-going shipbuilding techniques these craftsmen brought with them may have initially slowed the evolution of the steamboat. But as these men became familiar with the conditions of the western rivers, and as more westerners began to build steamboats, the long-held traditions of deep-draft, stoutly built ships were discarded in favor of the pragmatic job of building steamboats for the vastly different river conditions of the West. Burton Hazen, a ship-

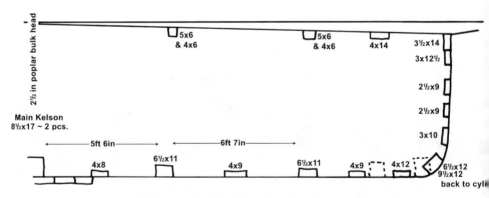

*4.3. A diagram detailing the cross-section of a steamboat to be built by the Howard Ship Yard and Dock Company in 1882.*

wright from Cincinnati, gave testimony during the Wheeling Bridge Case that sheds light on the adaptation of hull form to the western rivers: "We consider we have made considerable improvement in the model of the hulls of steamboats since 1830, in the form of the bottom of the vessel, making it flatter, fore and aft, than formerly, by which we get a lighter draft of water. Our models are somewhat sharper than they were, at the bow; by which we have increased the speed, and they are sharper at the water line. There is generally an increase of the length of floor; for the purpose of lightening the water draft. The size of the boats has increased; thereby the capacity for carrying has been increased. We build them likewise of much lighter timber; which increases the lightness of the draft."[5]

Hazen's remarks are reflected in the remains of the Red River Wreck, the earliest steamboat wreck yet located. The name of the vessel remains a mystery, however, its construction and the location of the wreck give significant clues as to its date. As the name indicates, it is located in the Red River above Shreveport, Louisiana. During the early years of steam navigation, steamboats could not ply the Red above Natchitoches, Louisiana, due to an immense accumulation of snags, drift logs, and floating trees. This 150-mile-long series of intermittent obstructions, known as the Great Raft, was not entirely cleared until 1838, indicating the wreck could not have sank before that date, though it may have been built before then. While most of the vessel's machinery was salvaged, evidence shows the boat had only one engine, indicative of steamboat construction before 1840.

The most important characteristic of the Red River Wreck lies in a construction feature and temporal indicator that its hull does not contain, namely hog chains. This advancement (believed to have occurred between 1835 and 1841) was the most significant innovation in the development of the western river steamboat. Hog chains were wrought-iron rods that ran the length of the hull, helping prevent hogging and sagging. This advancement allowed hulls to be built longer, shallower, and of lighter timbers. The Red River Wreck's hull is flat bottomed and lightly built, both features seen on later steamboats. But the fundamental difference in construction relative to later vessels is found in the keelson, bilge keelsons, and clamps. All of these fore-and-aft members are notched to fit securely over the floors and/or futtocks. The extensive

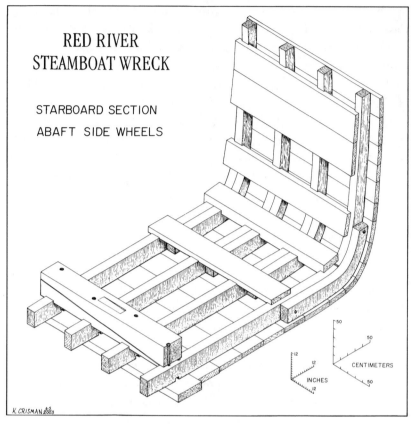

RED RIVER
STEAMBOAT WRECK

STARBOARD SECTION
ABAFT SIDE WHEELS

K. CRISMAN 2003

*4.4. An isometric drawing showing the flat-bottomed hull of the
Red River Wreck (34Ch280), a steamboat from about the 1830s.*

notching was undoubtedly a time-consuming endeavor, but it appears to
have lent significant longitudinal strength to the lightly built hull. The
length-to-breadth ratio for this steamboat is approximately 5.2:1 (considerably higher than that of traditional wooden oceangoing vessels),
indicating that the lengthening of the steamboat hull was well underway before the introduction of hog chains. The results of ongoing studies of this vessel (underway in 2003) should add substantially to the
understanding of steamboat construction during this important intermediate period.

Throughout the nineteenth century, western river steamboats were
normally custom built for the future owner. The contract for the con-

struction of the steamboat *Yellowstone* (1831) provides insight into construction practices during this period. Though many facets of *Yellowstone*'s construction had been adapted to western river conditions, its hull differed considerably from the fully developed steamboat of the 1840s; in this sense it was representative of other vessels built during the early 1830s.

*Yellowstone*'s hull had a length of 120 feet, a beam of 20 feet, and a depth of 6 feet, with a length-to-beam ratio of 6:1. The hull was quite shallow and almost certainly flat bottomed or nearly so, with the framing of the hull divided into three sections. The after portion of the hull had double frames, seven inches moulded and four inches sided, with room and space of twelve inches. The framing for the center of the vessel was composed of single frames, six inches sided and seven inches moulded. The floors were spaced seventeen inches on centers, with the

*4.5. A painting by George Catlin of the steamboat* Yellowstone, *built in 1831.*

futtocks let into the floors one inch. The framing at the bow was more robust to resist damage from snags and driftwood. Double frames were ordered for the forwardmost 50 feet of the hull, with the space between the frames reducing to only two inches within 15 feet of the stem. The bow was also equipped with a snag chamber "well fitted and caulked."[6]

The evolution of the steamboat's hull directly affected the development of its superstructure. During the early 1820s, the reduction of the depth of hold made that location an increasingly inconvenient space to house passengers. This diminished depth forced passenger accommodations to the main deck and above, with the hold being reserved for cargo. Henry Shreve was widely credited for being the first shipwright to build a vessel with an upper deck in his second boat, *George Washington* (1825), although an earlier craft, *Emerald* (1824), seems to have also had this feature. Identifying the exact vessel or builder to first employ this design innovation is beside the point; what is important is that regional shipwrights were presented with the same set of problems and constraints and, not surprisingly, derived similar solutions.[7]

By the mid-1820s, passengers were typically housed on both the main deck and the upper deck, more commonly known as the boiler deck. *Reindeer,* which ran in 1827–29, was described as having the gentlemen's cabin on the main deck, abaft the machinery, while the ladies' cabin occupied the after portion of the upper deck. The forward portion of the

*4.6. Henry Shreve's* George Washington, *built in 1825.*

upper deck was reserved for deck passengers. This arrangement quickly gave way to all of the cabin passengers being housed on the boiler deck, with the ladies' cabin abaft the gentlemen's cabin; deck passengers were forced to find accommodations among the cargo and machinery on the main deck. Each room was partitioned with either a curtain or a door, and all opened into a saloon, or long hallway, that ran the length of the boiler deck. The saloon was used as the dining room and was generally an area for interaction between the more privileged passengers. The outboard edge of the boiler deck was ringed by a gallery, an open walkway that served as an airy place of relaxation for the cabin passengers. On some steamboats, passenger rooms opened onto the gallery, while others had small hallways leading from the saloon to the gallery. The ceiling of the boiler deck was formed by the hurricane deck. This floor was slightly crowned to help it shed water and was either tarred or covered with waxed and varnished canvas.[8]

The upper deck of the steamboat was often decorated in elaborate fashion with intricate paintwork, expensive carpets, chandeliers, sofas, tables, and chairs. This was in stark contrast to the utilitarian look of the main deck. The disparity between the two decks was not lost on contemporaries. Traveling aboard a western river steamboat in 1838, David Stevenson observed that the after end of the lower deck, "which is covered in, and occupied by the crew of the vessel and the deck passengers, generally presents a scene of filth and wretchedness that baffles all description." By contrast, the upper deck was "fitted up in a gorgeous style; the berths are large, and the numerous windows by which the cabin is surrounded give abundance of light, and, what is of great consequence in that scorching climate, admit a plentiful supply of fresh air."[9]

*Machinery*

Throughout the 1820s, the diversity in steamboat boiler and engine designs declined, and machinery specifically developed to cope with the region's swift rivers and to take advantage of its plentiful fuel supplies became prominent. At the close of the decade, not only had the high-pressure engine become the dominant type used but also its positioning and design had developed into the general form it would retain for the remainder of the century. On pace with its progression overall, the steamboat's machinery evolved with tremendous rapidity. Within twenty

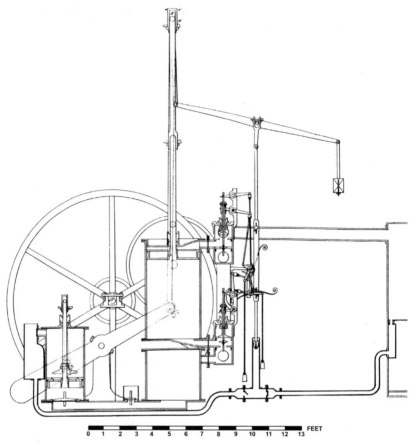

4.7. *A cross-section of the low-pressure condensing engine from the steamer* Robert Fulton.

years, the power plant was entirely revamped to suit the requirements of the western rivers.

The few steamboats powered by low-pressure engines during this period were largely of eastern manufacture. Several drawings show such systems used in the West during this period, the best drawing being that of *Robert Fulton*, built in New York City in 1819 and arriving in New Orleans in the spring of 1820. *Robert Fulton* had a length of 158 feet, a beam of 33 feet, a depth of hull of 10 feet, and was five hundred tons burden. Its single boiler was 30.8 feet long, 8.9 feet wide, and 8.9 feet high, and while the working pressure of this large boiler is not known, one can surmise from its boxlike shape that it was low. Heated by a single furnace, the boiler had four horizontal flues that ran to the back of the furnace, returned over themselves, and united at the smokestack. French marine engineer Jean Baptiste Marestier, in his account of *Robert Fulton,* does not specify the material used to construct the boilers. Given the vessel's oceanic journey and the rapid corrosion of iron when exposed to salt water, however, it is likely that copper was used. *Robert Fulton* carried a low-pressure, double-acting side-lever engine. The cylinder had a diameter of 3.7 feet and a piston stroke of 5 feet.[10]

By the mid-1820s the trend was clear; high-pressure engines were rapidly displacing their low-pressure counterparts. By 1830, the basic design and layout of the high-pressure engine was well established, yet contemporary testimony indicates there were still no standards or specifications in the details of its construction. This lack of standardization, combined with an absence of a steamboat-building tradition, facilitated continual improvement by machinists in all aspects of the engine. Such experimentation was implied by steamboat builder Reuben Miller in 1850, during his testimony in the Wheeling Bridge Case, regarding the construction of boilers when he revealed that there were no general rules in the construction of the furnace, the grate bars, the diameter of the

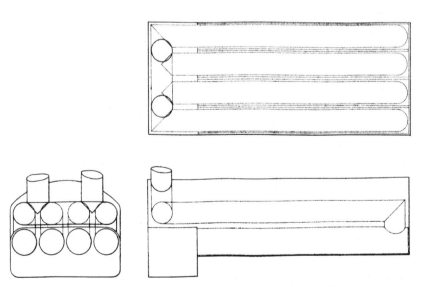

*4.8. The schematic drawings of the boiler of* Robert Fulton.

flues, or the diameter and length of the chimneys.[11] The infancy of steam technology allowed for experimentation, which produced uniquely adapted machinery over the course of just a few decades.

Given the conditions of western rivers, the high-pressure engine and shallow-draft, flat-bottomed hull were necessary characteristics of steamboats. The vessels had to not only draw minimal water but also stem rapids and occasionally deepen channels by plowing through riverbeds. The high-pressure engine was approximately 60 percent lighter than a low-pressure condensing engine, decreasing the overall weight of the steamboat and, likewise, its draft.[12] Additionally, the power supplied by the high-pressure engine was far superior. Although fuel consumption for the engine type was high, this drawback was relatively minor in light of the West's plentiful and inexpensive wood supply.

In 1860 Norman Russell, a British naval architect, noted that, in comparison to an ordinary condensing engine, the high-pressure engine of a western river steamboat was 60 percent cheaper.[13] This was due largely to its simplicity of design and lack of ornamentation. Furthermore, since boat engineers were not formally educated in steam engineering and there was a dearth of machine shops through much of the trans-Appalachian West, there was an added benefit due to the high-pressure steam engine's uncomplicated machinery: they were much easier to repair. Steamboats were often hundreds of miles from a city with significant industrial capabilities, so the capability to repair engines in the field was essential.

The straightforward nature of the high-pressure engine was better suited to the peculiarities of river navigation. In particular, the limber hulls of western steamboats constantly altered the alignment of the machinery. The simple high-pressure engine, not built with anything approaching precision, was more easily adjusted to these frequent changes than a well-made and accurately fitted low-pressure engine. Finally, the silty nature of river water was believed to more adversely affect low-pressure engines; the sediment contained in the steam accumulated in the condenser, rendering it inefficient and causing continual "vexation and annoyance."[14]

Testimony given by civil engineer Edwin F. Johnson during the Wheeling Bridge Case encapsulates the reasons and enthusiasm for the adoption of high-pressure engines during this period. "The conditions important to that navigation are lightness of draft of the boats, and a sufficient power in the engine to propel boats at the required speed. To this end it is essential that the engines with their appurtenances should have the least possible weight; this is attained by dispensing with the condensing apparatus and giving the cylindrical form to the boilers; so as to use, with greater safety, steam of a high pressure, in boilers of a small size and weight."[15]

The universal adoption of high-pressure steam machinery in the West was rarely viewed in a favorable light by outside observers, though. Critics in both the eastern United States and England, where low-pressure steam engines were commonly employed, often called this technology dangerous and wasteful, especially when applied by ignorant, reckless, western engineers. Writing in the *Journal of the Franklin Institute*, J. V. Merrick expressed the dissenting opinion held by many: "The Western steamboats are made on a peculiar type, which is to be found principally in that section of the country, and whose existence at this stage of improvement in river navigation only serves to show how far prejudice, and a spirit of servile imitation, can prevent advances dictated by science, or by successful experience elsewhere."[16] The high-pressure engines used on western steamboats were well adapted to the surrounding conditions but were much more dangerous and wasteful than low-pressure condensing engines.

Unfortunately, there are currently no known illustrations of the high-pressure engines used on the western river steamboats dating to the 1820s, however, there is an early depiction of a high-pressure engine used on eastern steamboats of this period. In general, western steamboats of this era were powered by one horizontally oriented poppet-valve engine located on the main deck. The cylinder was twelve to twenty inches in diameter, and the stroke of the piston was between three and five feet.[17] (The exact manner in which this type of engine functioned will be discussed in more detail in the following chapter.)

Technical literature regarding the design of western river steamboats is scarce, the notable exception to this being the documentation of high-pressure boilers. The tendency of boilers to explode, often taking many lives, placed them under public scrutiny again and again during the nineteenth century. The horrific loss of life with and the potential remedies for such accidents were investigated in numerous technical jour-

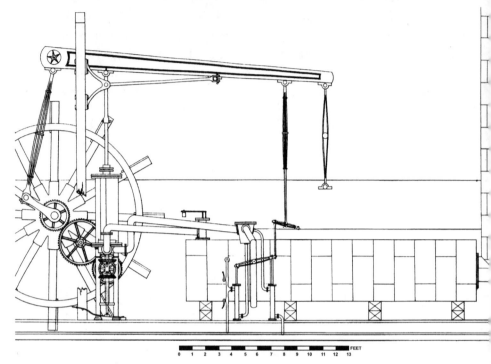

*4.9. An early high-pressure steamboat engine, much
like those used on vessels of the western rivers.*

nals and by Congress. A clear understanding of the power plant of the
western steamboat can be drawn from this information.

The cylindrical high-pressure boiler of this period was a direct de-
scendent of the type designed by Oliver Evans. Evans's *Abortion of the
Young Steam Engineer's Guide,* published in 1805, describes these boilers
as oriented horizontally and cylindrical in form, with a diameter not exceeding three feet. The amount of steam generated was increased by
either lengthening the boilers or by increasing their number. Two different designs were proposed for exposing the boiler surface to the heat
of the furnace. In the simpler and cheaper method, the furnace was set
at one end of the boiler and the flame was allowed to travel its full length.
The second design, which was adopted on the western rivers, was the

use of an internal flue. Evans believed that, although this latter design was expensive to construct, it would need only two-thirds as much fuel.[18]

Typical high-pressure boilers were long and cylindrical, positioned horizontally just forward of amidships on the main deck. They were constructed with little regard for efficiency, with minimum weight, bulk, and cost prevailing over all other qualities. They were revered by steamboat engineers for their ease of cleaning and repair and reviled by many others for their frequent explosions. The number and dimension of boilers varied over time as steam-engine builders experimented to find a design that combined minimum weight and cost with maximum strength and power. In the 1820s two to three boilers with diameters of eighteen inches and lengths of 18 feet were sufficient for powering a steamboat, but this soon increased. In 1831, steamboats typically had four or five boilers, each with lengths of 18–20 feet and diameters of 3 feet. In the mid-1830s the use of eight boilers with diameters of 3½ feet and lengths of 23 feet was not uncommon.[19]

Boilers, with very few exceptions in the earliest years of this period, were constructed of iron. Through the 1820s, boiler plates were wrought from solid slabs of iron worked together with a hammer. In the late 1820s, this process was altered so that the iron plates were made with the use of large rollers. Blooms of iron were heated by anthracite coal and worked under a large hammer into thick slabs. Each slab was put under a roller, first in the direction of the slab's longitudinal axis and then perpendicular to its first orientation. It was thus reduced in thickness to a large bar, which was then cut to the desired length and width; several bars were piled on top of each other and then passed again, at a high heat, under a roller. These were not welded together as with forged iron but soldered to each other by intervening layers of cast iron, with the belief that this would reduce imperfections in the plate. The assumption was that multiple layers allowed for any weak points in an individual iron sheet to be strengthened by adjacent sheets. The boiler shell was assembled of these rolled iron plates joined by rivets. These individual shells did not stand alone but were joined to others to create a battery of boilers. Each shell was connected to the adjacent shell by one or two large, concave cast-iron washers. The washers spanned the distance between each boiler, with their locations corresponding to a hole

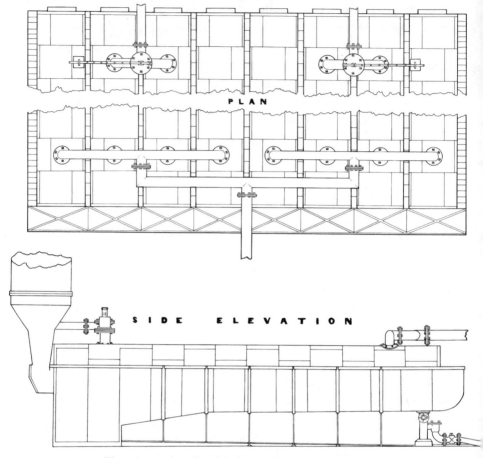

PLAN

SIDE ELEVATION

*4.10. Plan view and profile of the boilers of a western river steamboat, 1840.*

in each shell. This allowed for the free flow of water within the battery.[20] The boilers, once connected into a single unit, were held above the main deck by numerous wrought-iron tie rods, which spanned the distance from the main deck to the battery's base.

An iron boiler head sealed each end of the boiler. A boiler head was not a solid slab of metal but was pierced by several holes. One hole went through the head for each flue in the boiler. The exception to this was in the case of elbow flues (described below). Each boiler head was equipped with a manhead (and often with a little manhead as well). The manhead was an oval lid covering a hole in the boiler head and allowed a person to enter the unit in order to clean the inside. The little manhead was a smaller hole with a corresponding lid located at the bottom of the boiler head that allowed the water to be drained from the boiler as well as partial cleaning.[21]

Cast-iron heads were used throughout this period because of their ease of manufacture, but they were considered unsatisfactory in comparison to wrought-iron heads. Cast-iron heads were between ¾ and 2 inches thick, but air holes concealed in them during manufacture made them significantly weaker than they appeared. Furthermore, the repeated heating and cooling of cast iron damaged the metal, making it prone to cracking. These cracks often proved to be weak points when a boiler was filled with high-pressure steam. Moreover, when the flue collapsed, the shock from that process often broke the cast-iron head through which the flue passed. Whereas a wrought-iron head would tend to bend or tear, the cast-iron head's rigidity caused it to shatter. This resulted in fragments being propelled with great force during an explosion. Calls were repeatedly made to eliminate the use of cast-iron boiler heads on steamboats throughout this period, but it was not until the late 1840s when their use was entirely phased out.[22]

The use of flues was readily adopted on the western rivers. Flues were iron tubes running the length of the boiler's interior. These were open to the furnace, permitting hot gases to travel through them, thus providing a larger surface area for heating the water in the boilers. During the 1820s and 1830s, single-flue boilers were thirty-four to thirty-eight inches in diameter with a sixteen-to-twenty-inch-diameter flue. Double-flue boilers were thirty-six to forty inches in diameter with flues of twelve to seventeen inches in diameter. Both types of boilers were sixteen to twenty-two feet in length.[23]

Through the late 1820s, boilers were equipped with one flue, but preference was soon given to two flues. Different were not only the sizes of these single and double flues but also their constructions. Single flues did not exit the boiler through the boiler head as did double flues. They were known as elbow or L-flues because, in the forward part of the boiler, they made a ninety-degree turn upward, exiting through the top of the boiler. This feature was believed to be the cause of several boiler explosions. The bend in this type was not covered by water as was the rest of the flue. This prevented the exposed portion from being cooled by the water, becoming red hot and frequently losing its ability to with-stand the steam pressure. In these instances the flue would collapse, often with catastrophic results.[24]

Although elbow flues were especially prone to collapsing, all styles in-troduced an element of weakness into the boiler. A flue ran through the center of the boiler and thus was exposed if the water level inside dropped too low; without this coolant, the flue became red hot. Two un-pleasant outcomes often resulted from this situation: either the heat from the furnace would cause the flue to become malleable and col-lapse, thus exploding the boiler, or the low water level would be discov-ered and more added to remedy the deficiency. This second action re-sulted in a dramatic increase in steam pressure from the instantaneous vaporization of the water when it hit the red-hot flue. Sometimes the boilers would hold; sometimes they would not.

Regardless of flue type, the juncture between it and the boiler or the boiler head was secured in the same manner. The end of the flue had a flange or washer around its end. These were punctuated with rivet holes corresponding with the holes in the boiler or the boiler head. The junc-ture of these two pieces of metal was made steam-tight with lead grum-mets or collars sandwiched between the two pieces of riveted iron.[25]

Throughout the development of the western river steamboat, boilers were equipped with two basic safety devices: gauge cocks and safety valves.[26] Gauge cocks were three small valves located one above the other on the boiler head. They were positioned just below, equal to, and above the desired water level. The valves were opened with a gauge stick (typically a broom handle): if water flowed when the highest gauge was opened, the supply was cut off; if water flowed from the middle but not the upper gauge, a normal supply was in the boiler; if only the lower gauge exhausted water, then more was added. According to George Merrick, a cub engineer, if all of the gauge cocks were dry, "there fol-lowed a guessing match as to just how far below the minimum the water really was, and what would be the result of throwing in a supply of cold water. The supply was always thrown in, and that quickly, as time counts in such cases." Gauge cocks were widely acknowledged to be an impre-cise indicator of a boiler's water level. The release of steam pressure by the opening of the gauge cock often caused the water in the boiler to foam, giving a false impression of its true level.[27]

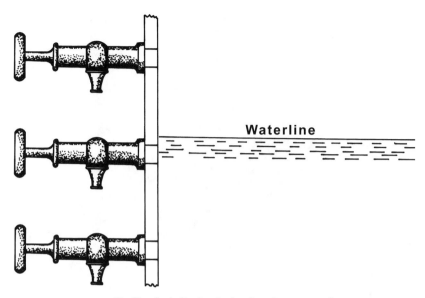

*4.11. Profile of a boiler head, showing the gauge cocks.*

Even from the earliest period, western steamboats were equipped with one or sometimes two safety valves, which were relatively small. In 1831 only half of them were more than one-half the size of the engine's throttle valve, and no more than a third of steamboats were equipped with more than one. They were also the subject of much controversy, for they tended only to create a false sense of security. Simply constructed, a safety valve consisted of a lever with an adjustable weight that, in theory, allowed the amount of steam pressure held inside the boiler to be adjusted. When enough steam built up to open the safety valve(s), the opening, generally only three to five inches in diameter, could often not expel enough to avoid an explosion. In fact, the sudden release of pressure would bring about a rapid expansion of steam in the boiler, frequently more than the valve could vent, resulting in an explosion actually caused by the safety valve. Most observers believed that these valves had "no more tendency to prevent an explosion than the touch hole of a cannon has to prevent it from bursting."[28]

Adding to the dangers of this design flaw was the often reckless weighting of the safety valve. The amount of steam pressure carried in the boiler, which was left entirely to the discretion of the engineer, was an

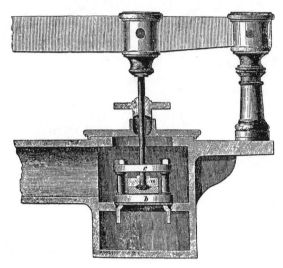

*4.12. A cross-section of a safety valve.*

issue of much controversy. Safety valves were held down by a moveable weight, called the pea, on a lever known as the death hook. The death hook was so named because of the habit of some engineers to weight it excessively in order to increase boiler pressure, thereby supplying the engine with more power. This was said to be a very common practice, with engineers frequently placing "twice as much weight [on the death hook] as the steam can raise when the boat is under way." This practice was frowned upon, especially in light of the fact that engineers were rarely educated in their trade, and scarcely one in twenty could actually calculate the amount of weight on the death hook relative to the pressure it withheld in the boiler. Another method of holding the safety valve down involved bracing a board between the safety-valve lever and an overhead beam. Engineers considered this technique better than a weight on the death hook because a weighted lever could still lift, causing the boiler to lose its water, while the board absolutely prevented this from happening. Repeated protests were made by observers from the 1820s through the 1840s demanding that at least one safety valve be locked in such a way that the engineer could not access it or to impose heavy fines for overweighting it.[29]

Steam-pressure gauges, despite their apparent necessity, were not common on western river steamboats. Open-tube mercury gauges had long been available for low-pressure boilers, but the excessive height of the column of mercury required to measure the steam pressure in a high-pressure boiler prevented widespread use of such gauges. The invention of the Bourdon bent-tube gauge in 1845 provided an adequate pressure instrument, but western engineers were slow to adopt these expensive, complicated new technologies. In 1852 Samuel Gilman noted that only a minority of steamboats carried steam gauges, the actual working pressure of most boilers being mere conjecture.[30]

Essential to the operation of the steam plant was a means of filling the boilers with water. This was accomplished with a water pump that took its motion from the engine. This feed pump worked well as long as the engine was in motion. But when the engine stopped, the pump also stopped supplying water to the boilers. For short stays this was often not a problem, but if the engines were halted for any greater length of time, the water level in the boilers could become dangerously low. This was overcome by throwing the paddle wheels out of gear so that the engines could continue to work without propelling the vessel. This was a wasteful and inconvenient technique, and frequently the fire in the furnace was not damped during stops, allowing the steam merely to vent through the engine cylinders. In this way the water supply in the boilers was rapidly depleted, potentially exposing the flues to the heated gases from the furnace without the water's cooling effect. When the engine was again set in motion, cold water would be forced into the boilers. The water on the red-hot flues would instantly vaporize, causing an abrupt rise in steam pressure and all too frequently an explosion as well.[31]

Boilers were connected to each other by several drums, both above and below. Located above and perpendicular to the battery of boilers, the steam drum served to collect the steam before passing to power the engine. It was cylindrical and constructed of plate iron similar to the boiler shell. The mud drum was of similar construction and orientation but was located below the boiler. This device was first used on the western rivers in the late 1820s and was subsequently incorporated into the machinery of all regional steamboats. The iron cylinder made boiler cleaning less frequent since sediment accumulated in it and could be removed via a blow-off valve several times a day.[32]

The fire was generated in the furnace at the forward end of the boilers. The position of the furnace, combined with the longitudinally oriented boilers, created a strong natural draft.[33] Access was through the furnace doors, located in between each pair of boilers. The grate, upon which fuel was placed, averaged four feet in depth and spanned the combined width of all the boilers. Openings between each grate bar varied from ⅝ inch for coal to 1 inch for wood.[34]

A casing of sheet iron encompassed all of the furnace and the bottom half of the boilers. This feature was designed to keep the heat in contact with the boilers and to force the furnace gases through the flues and into the chimneys. The casing was typically 3/16 inch thick, though frequently thicker at the after end, or back wall, and at the forward end, or breeching. The breeching was the intermediate stage between the casing and the chimneys, collecting the gases from the numerous flues and transferring them to one of the two chimneys. It was equipped with doors to allow access to the boiler heads and through them to the boilers.[35]

The tops of the boilers were not covered by the casing but were generally insulated by some other means. Contemporary accounts describe mixtures of plaster or clay, but Bates notes that many other materials, such as asbestos, firebrick, fireclay, and combinations of manure, straw, and earth, were also applied.[36]

Although located on the main deck, the boilers did not rest on the deck itself. A single layer of brick, laid flat, was placed on the deck to insulate it from the heat of the furnace. The edge of the fire bed would be made more pronounced by laying the end bricks on their sides.[37]

The boilers of western river steamboats, though exempt from the corrosion problems caused by salt water, were subject to the drawbacks of using silt-laden river water. Sediment and plant debris accumulated quickly and needed to be removed. This was partially accomplished by opening the valves of the mud drum, allowing accumulated sediment to blow out. Although this cleared much of the sediment from the bottoms of the boilers, it did not entirely clean them, for not all of the sediment accumulated in the mud drum; the remainder formed a dense deposit in the bottom of the boiler. This deposit, often described as being bricklike in density, tended to reduce the heat transfer from the furnace to the water. Another drawback to using river water was the dissolved minerals and salts it contains. These compounds had the potential to form a crust on the boiler and flues to the effect of sealing them off from contact with the water.[38] Lacking this contact, the iron could become red hot and rupture.

Whether from accumulated sediment or mineral deposits, boilers required frequent cleaning to stay in peak working order. This unpleasant job was conducted several times per journey, normally by a cub engineer. The experience of George Merrick accurately characterizes this task:

Being a slim lad, one of my duties was to creep into the boilers through the manhole, which was just large enough to let me through; and with a hammer and a sharp-linked chain I must "scale" the boilers by pounding on the two large flues and the sides with the hammer, and sawing the chain around the flues until all the accumulated mud and sediment was loosened. Scaling boilers was what decided me not to persevere in the engineering line. To lie flat on one's stomach on the tip of a twelve-inch flue, studded with rivet heads, with a space of only fifteen inches above one's head, and in this position haul a chain back and forth without any leverage whatever, simply by the muscles of the arm, with the thermometer 90° in the shade, was a practice well calculated to disillusionize any one not wholly given over to mechanics.[39]

The hard work of the engines and boilers was most visible in the turning of the paddle wheels. Throughout the nineteenth century, paddle wheels were the exclusive method used to propel western river steamboats. They had several advantages over the obvious alternative, the screw propeller. Most significantly, working propellers were not available until about 1840, long after the hull form and machinery of the steamboats were well established. Even after the successful application of propeller technology on the Great Lakes and elsewhere, the use of this machinery on western rivers presented nearly insurmountable problems. Early propeller shafts were prone to leaks, for the river sediment damaged their watertight seals. These joints and seals were difficult to repair, especially given the lack of facilities for dry-docking vessels.[40] Moreover, the propellers on large vessels required a considerable depth of water often not available of western rivers. In these shallow channels propellers were vulnerable to snags, and once damaged, their repair required specialized tools not found in ordinary machine shops.

In contrast, paddle wheels (as developed on the western rivers) were consistent with other trends seen in the construction of this type of steamboat. Paddle wheels were relatively uncomplicated and inexpensive devices that could be maintained without access to machine shops or iron foundries. The design's simplicity made it easy to repair, an essential feature given that paddle wheels were commonly damaged by floating debris and steamboats were often hundreds of miles from urban centers. All of the parts were above the level of the water for most of the wheel's revolution, which eliminated problems associated with watertight seals and made repairs much easier to conduct. Paddle wheels, however, did have significant drawbacks. In comparison to propellers, they were massively heavy, an unfortunate detraction given that shipwrights were continually trying to decrease the draft of their vessels. They were also quite inefficient, with the shower of water they lifted out of the river representing wasted fuel and money.[41] Neither of these detractions, however, was significant enough to outweigh the advantages.

Positioning the paddle wheels at the sides of the steamboat was preferred during this period. In the 1820s, they were frequently located amidships or slightly forward of this point, but as time progressed, the trend was to move the wheels farther aft. By the middle to late 1830s, they had been moved one-quarter to one-third the length of the vessel forward of the transom. For side-wheelers, this position would be maintained for the remainder of the nineteenth century.

Throughout the 1820s and 1830s, paddle wheels grew in width and diameter. By enlarging the diameter, the rotary speed of the wheel was increased with only modest additional energy consumption. As the diameter increased, the height of the cylinder timbers upon which the wheel shaft rested was raised. This resulted in the cylinder being angled upward so that the pitman could rotate the shaft.

A feature of western steamboats that became more prominent during this period were the chimneys. These rose from the forward end of the boilers and were connected to them via the breeching. Well-made chimneys were essential to the proper firing of the boiler and therefore the power of the engine. They carried the smoke and soot away from the vessel and, in the process, created a natural draft in the furnace. As the heated gases rose inside the confined space of the stack, they forced a flow of air, the draft, into the furnace to fill the drop in pressure. This forced oxygen into the furnace, accelerating the combustion of fuel. A secondary consideration in the construction of the chimneys was aesthetics. Although certainly not the primary feature, tall stacks were seen as improving the looks of a vessel, and certain observers asserted that this was the sole reason for the towering chimneys of later vessels.[42]

As with many features of the steamboat, chimneys grew in both diameter and height throughout this period. In 1850 a veteran steamboat commander estimated that in 1820 the average chimney was approximately fourteen feet high from the center of the flues, with a diameter of about twelve inches. By the early 1830s, chimneys typically rose twenty-five to forty-five feet from the flues and were twenty-five to forty inches in diameter. One limiting factor regarding the height of chimneys was the tendency for taller structures to cause vessels to roll.[43] As the average breadth of steamboat hulls increased through the 1840s and 1850s, this problem would be largely overcome.

Chimneys were built of multiple sections of sheet iron, each known as a ring, riveted to each other. Unlike the steamboats of the later nineteenth century, the tops of chimneys in this period typically were not decorated. But the tops of some vessels were equipped with "a semi circular sieve, in the form of a ball," intended to extinguish sparks as they exited.[44] The use of this device was discontinued later because it diminished the draft of the furnace.

From 1820 through 1835, western-river-steamboat design underwent major adaptive developments. Most importantly, hulls became shallower and more flat bottomed. As a consequence, passenger accommodations were moved above the waterline. Structural improvements were paralleled by advances in the design of engines and boilers, with the light and powerful high-pressure steam engine being universally adopted.

## COLONIZING THE WEST
### STEAMBOATS, 1835-60

*On account of the great fluctuations in the depth of water and the strength*
*of the current, it is necessary that the boat be built light and with a full*
*model, that its immersion may not be too great for low stages of water in the*
*river; and at the same time the boat should have great power with but little*
*weight, and the model should be such as to be easy of propulsion, to be*
*enabled to ascend the rapids, —conditions, all of which is not easy to satisfy.*
Thomas Tredgold, *The Principles and Practice and Explanation*
*of the Machinery Used in Steam Navigation, Volume II, Part I*

During the late 1830s, the structural and mechanical development of
the western river steamboat was essentially completed. Earlier vessels
were deep-drafted, heavily built ships, but by the mid-1830s the standard became shallow, lightly constructed, flat-bottomed boats with multiple decks rising high above the waterline, a form retained for the remainder of the century. The steamboat's evolution was not the result of
great leaps in technology or leaps of creative genius, but of incremental
improvements in hull form and machinery by countless shipwrights, engineers, and mechanics. These advances were reflected in the its ability
to carry more freight and passengers on less water than any other class
of steamboat in the world. Moreover, the cost of construction per ton of
freight, capacity, and passenger accommodation was less than any other
type of steamer.[1]

The structural analysis of western steamboats of this period is greatly
aided by archaeological data. These studies provide the best glimpse
possible into steamboat construction. The most significant structural
variation among these vessels relates to paddle wheel placement. As indicated by their names, side-wheelers had dual wheels, one on each side
of the hull approximately one-third of the vessel's length forward of the

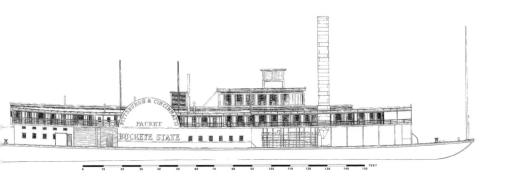

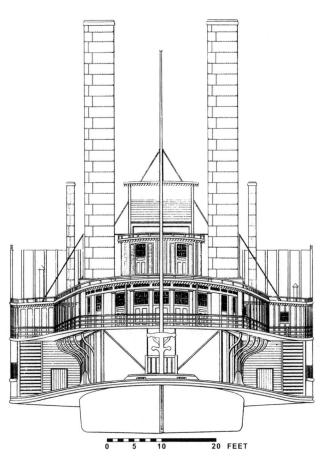

5.1. and 5.2. These two views show the Buckeye State (1850), a typical western river packet steamboat of this era. She was a side-wheeler whose hull was built in Shousetown, Pennsylvania, and sent to Pittsburgh for the installation of her machinery and completion of the superstructure. The vessel had a length of 260 feet; a beam of 29 feet, 5 inches; and a depth of 6½ feet. These drawings represent the earliest detailed schematics of a western river steamboat known to exist.

stern. Stern-wheelers had a single wheel that projected aft beyond the lines of the hull. During the antebellum period, side-wheelers were the dominant type, though progressively less so as the Civil War approached. Although stern-wheelers represent a very important chapter in the history of the western river steamboat, this study focuses primarily on the construction of the side-wheel steamboat. Nevertheless, an overview of the basic development of the stern-wheel steamboat is instructive.

Mounting the paddle wheel at the stern was quite common during the first fifteen years of steam navigation on the western rivers, but these precursors bore little resemblance to those vessels developed during this period. Early stern-wheelers had relatively small wheels set within the lines of the hull, known as a bootjack hull. This positioning restrained the size of the paddle wheel, especially in terms of breadth, and took up significant space in the hull. Furthermore, the weight of the paddle wheel and the consequent reduction of buoyancy of the stern made the hull prone to hogging. Because of these structural problems, early stern-wheelers were superceded by side-wheelers in the 1820s. It was not until the 1840s that stern-wheelers again became an unexceptional sight on the western rivers. Writing in 1842, an English observer noted: "In the course of our progress we saw two or three small steamers with their paddle-wheel at the stern instead of at the sides; there being only one wheel, right in the center over the stern. By this, it is said, they are propelled in a straight course, almost as rapidly as by two at the sides; but it renders them difficult to steer, though, adding nothing to the breadth of the vessels, they are less liable to get foul of each other."[2] In the following decades the number of stern-wheelers steadily increased until they effectively replaced side-wheelers in the postbellum period.

Placing a single paddle-wheel at the stern had two major advantages over positioning one port and starboard. First, the shape of a steamboat's hull tended to push any flotsam it encountered to the side. Thus, on side-wheelers, debris would be forced straight into the paddle wheel. In contrast, a paddle wheel at the stern was mostly sheltered from debris floating in the river; driftwood damage was thereby largely eliminated, leading to fewer repairs during a journey. The second and most material advantage of stern-wheelers was their lower draft compared with side-wheelers of equal tonnage. When paddle wheels were mounted at the sides, the overall breadth of the main deck was increased by the width of the wheels via the guards, the decking supported by outrigger beams projecting outside the lines of the hull. Side-wheelers during this period typically had guards with widths that were 50–75 percent of the breadth of the hull. Although these were used for cargo space on the main deck, their overall width was determined by that of the paddle wheels. Thus, the buoyancy of the hull was constrained by the necessity of always having to extend the breadth of the main deck by a width equal to that of the paddle wheels. Stern-wheelers, however, generally had either small guards or none at all. Their length-to-breadth ratio was less than that of side-wheelers, with a corresponding increase in the buoyancy of the hull for a given length. This was particularly important for western river steamboats because the length of a vessel's navigation season was dependent on the amount of water its hull drew. Stern-wheelers, which could run on shallower water, could service a greater area for more of the year. This advantage became paramount as competition from railroads increased.

The major structural disadvantage of stern-wheelers was hull distortion caused by placing the paddle wheel so far aft. This tremendous weight compounded the tendency for steamboat sterns to hog, an insurmountable problem before the successful employment of hog chains in the late 1830s and early 1840s; it was no coincidence that stern-wheelers came into favor shortly thereafter. Side-wheelers were braced by one longitudinal hog chain, while the predisposition for stern-wheel steamboat hulls to distort required the use of two sets of longitudinal hog chains, with two additional sets of chains just to support the paddle wheel.

*Structure*

Through experimentation, western shipwrights learned that long, narrow, flat-bottomed hulls were better suited to the rapid currents and shallow waters of the region's rivers. This design displaced the largest amount of water possible, allowing steamboats to "keep as nearly as possible upon the surface of the water." Longer vessels were faster than shorter boats of similar tonnage, for the extra length caused little additional resistance in the water relative to a comparable gain in cargo capacity. A long, full hull also increased the vessel's buoyancy and

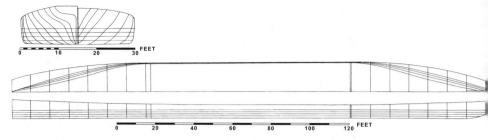

5.3. *Sheer, half-breadth, and body plan of* Buckeye State.

decreased its draft. This permitted boats to sail in shallower waters and consequently increased their profitability, for the length of a steamboat's running season was inversely proportional to its draft.[3]

The construction of the bow, much like the construction of the rest of the steamboat, was determined by river conditions. Widely varying water levels created impediments to the loading and unloading of passengers and freight. Seasonal fluctuations made permanent docks impractical because they would intermittently be either inundated by or too far above the river. Many landings and towns employed wharf boats or floating docks that were moored by rope, chain, or cable to mooring rings or posts located far up the bank. The wharf boat would be pulled up the bank as the river rose, and alternately, as the river dropped, it was sparred out to deeper water. Wharf boats, however, were too expensive for less frequented landings. Instead, the bow of the steamboat was designed with a long, rounded rake to accommodate the vessel being eased up onto muddy riverbanks. Once the bow had ridden up onto the bank, a plank was quickly put out to the shore and the steamboat was secured to a nearby tree or mooring post.[4]

Although the rake of a steamboat bow tended to be long and rounded, its overall form was subject to variation. Jack Custer identifies three varieties: the model bow, the scow bow, and the spoonbill bow.[5] The model bow was the standard form used during this period (see, for example, fig. 5.3). It was generally employed on packets, the owners of which made much of their livelihood carrying passengers. Speed was important in this trade; therefore, the model bow was designed to cut through the water. The entrance was sharp, moving water cleanly along the outboard edges of the hull.

The scow bow was employed to some extent during this period; a bow of this type has been documented on *Cremona* (1852). In this form the entire flat bottom of the vessel's hull raked up at the bow. Not intended for speed, steamboats with scow hulls had to be pushed through the water rather than cutting through it. For vessels intended for trades in which speed was not a primary consideration, this style had several advantages. It was inexpensive and easy to build and repair. The scow bow was simply an extension of the flat-bottomed portion of the hull, only raked upward. This full form aided in lowering the draft of the vessel by increasing the surface area of the bow below the water.[6] Scow bows were employed more extensively in the late nineteenth and early twentieth centuries.

The spoonbill bow was used by many freight boats or low-water boats, though use of this style did not become widespread until around 1870. The spoonbill shape, with its wide, full entrance, placed more of the bow in the water. This increased buoyancy, correspondingly reducing the draft of the steamboat. The spoonbill's full form also made it less

*5.4. A photograph of a spoonbill bow under construction.*

prone to cutting into riverbanks when landing, making it easier to pull off the bank.

Generally, a steamboat bow was more heavily built than any other part of the hull. One or more breast hooks and yokes, heavy transverse beams, were used to stiffen it against both landing on riverbanks and encountering driftwood or ice while traveling.[7] The frames at the bow also had less room and space but with larger dimensions than those in any other portion of the hull. Even this staunch framing, however, did little to stop snags from puncturing the boat. Interestingly, the building of snag chambers in steamboat bows seems to have ceased during the late 1830s, despite the continued significant threat from snags.

The sterns of side-wheelers differed in nearly every aspect of their construction from those of stern-wheelers and were the most complex portion of the hull to build. Starting from about the beginning of the aft quarter of the vessel, the hull form was altered from its rectangular shape to a much narrower form, with the frames having considerable deadrise. In addition to this, the frames also arched outward, creating a hollow in the lines of the hull. The fine lines of the stern served to minimize turbulence around the single, large rectangular rudder, giving the vessel more maneuverability. The after end was marked by a counter stern, within which the sternpost and rudder post were contained.

In contrast to the sharp lines of side-wheeler sterns, those of stern-wheelers were full and generally much simpler to construct. It was built by raking the full, flat shape of the bottom of the hull upward just before it reached the transom. This increased the buoyancy of the stern, an important feature given the immense weight of the paddle wheel. The transom spanned most of the breadth of the hull and was oriented vertically. In later decades the sterns of stern-wheelers became more complicated, with the addition of complex steering systems and hull shapes, but prior to 1860 they remained relatively uncomplicated.

The superstructures of steamboats during this period contained three decks: main, boiler, and hurricane. Atop the hurricane deck was a cabin known as the Texas, above which was the pilothouse. These multiple decks, stacked upon one other, gave the western river steamboat its distinctive wedding cake–like appearance. These vessels looked distinctly top-heavy; between three-fourths and four-fifths of their total structural area was actually above the waterline. This apparent imbal-

5.5. *A photograph of the stern of the side-wheeler*
Liberty *(1900) while under construction.*

ance was lessened, however, by the placement of the machinery and
cargo on the main deck and, in the case of cargo, in the hold.[8] All of
the decks shared a number of features. Each had a slight camber, a modest rise toward the center of the deck helped drain water and improved
the looks of the vessel. The camber of the main deck also increased
space in the hold, an important feature for shallow-draft vessels. All
of the decks also had a modest sheer both fore and aft, which ranged
from four to five feet on large cotton packets to one foot or less on low-
water boats.

The main deck was the largest and most open of the decks. (The
upper half of figure 5.7 shows the layout of the main deck of *Buckeye
State*.) The main deck housed all of the machinery, heads, a blacksmith's
shop, bunks for deck passengers, and hatchways to the hold. It was the
primary storage area for the steamboat's cargo and the area to which
deck passengers were limited.

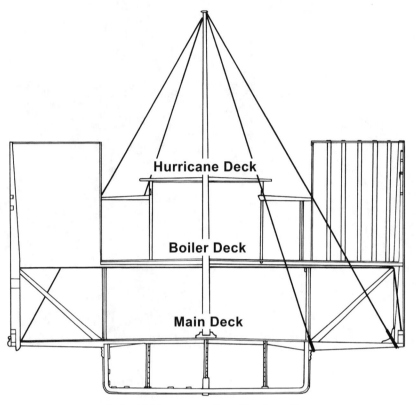

*5.6. A midships cross-section of* Buckeye State, *showing the main, boiler, and hurricane decks.*

The boiler deck, which had a width equal to the main deck, was used for the accommodation of cabin passengers. (The lower half of figure 5.7 illustrates the layout of *Buckeye State*'s boiler deck.) The bulk of this deck was composed of individual cabins for passengers and a saloon, the long central hallway, which extended the length of the deck. It also contained the pantry, men's and women's washrooms, the bar, and a baggage room. The entire exterior of the deck was ringed with a walkway, allowing access to fresh air without descending to the main deck.

The hurricane deck formed the roof of the boiler deck and was mostly open. The open portion held skylights, which illuminated the saloon below. The forward portion of the hurricane deck had a series of cabins that accommodated the crew and occasionally passengers as well.

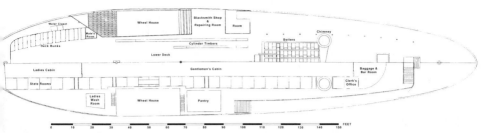

*5.7. This plan view of* Buckeye State *shows the layout of the main deck in the upper half and boiler deck in the lower half.*

This series of cabins, known as the Texas, was instituted in the early 1840s. The Texas was originally an odd, boxlike attachment atop the hurricane deck, but in the following decades it was gradually lengthened until it spanned approximately one-third of the vessel's length.[9] The pilothouse was either located atop the Texas or was a boxlike addition on its forward end. Ringed with windows, it gave the pilots a commanding view of their surroundings.

The design of the western steamboat's hull was both its greatest asset and its most significant drawback. As previously discussed, the hull was very shallow, long, and lightly built. John M. Sweeney asserts that they were "constructed with all the lightness in any way consistent with safety against falling to pieces." Not surprisingly, this structure had problems with hogging and sagging. Hull deformations had the potential to increase a steamboat's draft, open up planking seams, throw machinery out of alignment, and twist or rupture steam and water lines.[10] The limberness of the hull, however, was also an asset, for they needed to be flexible enough to avoid permanent damage from temporary deformations from groundings, sinkings, or impacts with submerged objects. Engineers lessened the tendency for steamboat hulls to distort, while maintaining their limberness, through several means. First, the position of the machinery (on side-wheelers) placed all of the weight from the boilers, paddle wheels, and engines about amidships, where the hull was most buoyant. This pushed the center of the hull down while lifting the bow and stern. Second, longitudinal bulkheads in the hold resisted the tendency to hog, or droop at the bow and stern. The import of these two techniques, however, were minor in comparison to hog chains.

*5.8. The steamboats* Car of Commerce *and* Embassy, *from a section of plate 2 in Fontayne's* The Cincinnati Panorama of 1848.

As with most advances in western river steamboat technology, the first vessel to employ hog chains remains unknown, yet there is no question that hog chains were the most significant structural development in the history of western-river-steamboat construction. (Louis Hunter's analysis of length-to-depth ratios suggests this advancement took place between 1835 and 1841.)[11] Hog chains were not chains at all but iron rods that ran the length of the vessel with the ends attached to the bottom of the hull. The central portion of the chain was carried on the tops of braces, or Sampson posts, just below the boiler deck. The tension on the chain was adjusted with turnbuckles, allowing for continual lifting of the ends of the hull. Hog chains maintained the shape of the hull, but just as importantly, they allowed construction with still lighter timbers. They also removed the need for heavy, staunch, longitudinal stiffeners in the hull, allowing it to be more limber. Finally, hog chains allowed the

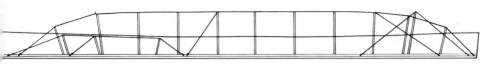

5.9. *A longitudinal cross-section of* City of New Orleans, *a side-wheeler built by the Howard Ship Yard and Dock Company in 1881, showing its trussing.*

steamboat to "work and strain freely," with captains reporting that boats would "work up and down two feet at every stroke of the engine."[12] Shipwrights now needed only to build a hull that would hold itself together, not one that had to retain its shape.

Side-wheelers typically had one hog chain running along the centerline of the vessel, while stern-wheelers, because of the excessive weight from the paddle wheel at the stern, had two offset chains. On side-wheelers, the after end of the hog chain was mounted into the keelson just forward of the sternpost, while the forward end was fastened one-quarter of the vessel's length aft of the stem. The forward ends of the hog chains of sternwheelers were mounted into bilge keelsons approximately one-quarter of the vessel's length aft of the stem. The aft ends of the chains applied tension to the cylinder timbers, which on stern-wheelers projected well past the transom. On both types of vessels, the chains were supported by braces mounted into the bottom of the hull. On side-wheelers, these braces rose to a level just below the boiler deck, while they extended above the boiler deck on many stern-wheelers. The braces in the aft end of the vessel angled in that direction, while those forward angled toward the bow.

Not only were steamboats susceptible to longitudinal hogging, but the additional weight on the sides of the hull from the guards, superstructure, and (on side-wheelers) the paddle-wheel assemblies also presented the secondary problem of transverse hogging. This tendency was restrained by cross and knuckle chains, which were similar in design to hog chains but were smaller in diameter. Cross chains were used to support the extremities of the guards, which tended to droop toward the water. Knuckle chains were used to support the sharp bilges, which accepted a great deal of downward force from the superstructure. Both cross and knuckle chains were carried on the top of vertically oriented braces positioned on or next to the keelson. Through the careful

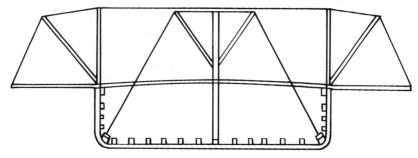

*5.10. This transverse cross-section of* City of New Orleans
*depicts her cross chains and knuckle chains.*

arrangement of these devices, the chains effectively lifted the sagging
portions of the hull, while the braces, via the downward pressure exerted by the chains that passed over them, pressed down on parts of the
hull that tended to lift.[13] By instituting these various trussing systems,
shipwrights were able to limit steamboat hogging while maintaining the
hull's limberness.

The invention of hog chains modified all of the internal structures
of the hull. Most of the archaeological examples of western river steamboats date to the years after the invention of hog chains; their hulls
were a marvel of construction. The following sections highlight basic
structural features found during the investigations of these vessels.
This discussion is necessarily weighted toward steamboat hulls since,
at the time of this writing, only two investigations have located parts of
the superstructure.[14]

Before delving into the particular construction features of steamboat
hulls, it is appropriate to mention the types of wood used in their construction. The archaeological record thus far supports the historical
literature in that the principal shipbuilding woods for western river
steamboats were white oak (*Quercus alba*) and white pine (*Pinus strobes*).
White oak was used for most hull components, including the keel, stem,
sternpost, framing, keelson, planking, stringers, clamps, deck beams,
and stanchions. White oak is generally heavy, hard, stiff, resistant to rot,
and has superior shock-resisting abilities. These qualities made white
oak the most sought-after shipbuilding timber for nineteenth-century
shipwrights. Moreover, white oak was also widely available in the trans-

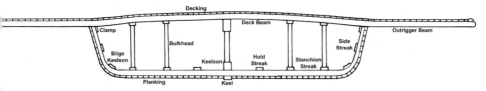

*5.11. A typical steamboat cross-section with the names of structural features.*

Appalachian West. Even as late as the 1880s, the forests of the Ohio River valley contained a supply of white oak exceeding that of the rest of the country put together. White pine was used for building the superstructure, decking, and bulkheads. This wood's characteristics include its light weight, low strength, straight grain, and moderate rot resistance. Although white oak and white pine were the two primary steamboat-building woods, there were a number of other species that have been found archaeologically or noted in primary sources. Three examples are yellow pine (*Pinus spp.*), for structural members and decking; yellow poplar (*Liriodendron tulipifera*), for building the superstructure; and cedar, for decking (*Chamaecyparis thyoides*), and it is highly likely that further steamboat investigations will find many exceptions to the exclusive use of white oak and white pine.[15]

KEEL

The building of a western steamboat began with the laving of its keel. The keel is defined as the lowest and strongest principal member of the hull that continues the full length of the vessel. In sailing ships, a heavy keel was the main longitudinal timber, helping counter the hogging or sagging of the hull. Because it projected below the bottom of the hull, the keel also helped counter leeway, the tendency for sailing vessels to be pushed in the direction of the wind when traveling windward.

The traditional functions of a keel were not only of no use to western steamboats but also detrimental. Flexibility was a requirement for steamboat hulls, given the frequent groundings to which they were prone. A stoutly built keel would counter the hull's flexibility. Deep keels also increased the amount of water a vessel drew, leading to more-frequent groundings and a shorter operating season for boats plying shallow rivers. Countering leeway was unnecessary for vessels powered exclusively by steam. Finally, a protruding keel hampered the sideways maneuverability of the steamboat, which was achieved through the manipulation of the rudder and both paddle wheels.[16]

Steamboat keels were more accurately keel planks.[17] They extended no more than one or two inches below the bottom of the hull and had a significantly larger sided dimension than moulded. Deep keels were likely given up early in the development of the western river steamboat. It seems likely that early shipwrights put an emphasis on the keelson, an internal longitudinal structural feature, rather than on a deeply projecting keel. Any strengthening of the keelson, however, was abandoned with the advent of hog chains, which provided the structural strength imparted by a heavy keel (or keelson) to counter hogging and sagging.

Among the seventeen archaeologically investigated steamboats, four contain specific information about the keel's construction. The sidewheeler *Kentucky* had a keel plank, moulded three inches and sided ten inches. The top of the keel was flush with the inboard face of the garboards, and the keel projected one inch below the bottom of the hull. The other three vessels, *Scotland, Cremona,* and *Bertrand,* lacked even a keel plank; the plank running along the centerline of the vessel differed in no way from the remainder of the planking.

STEM AND STERNPOST

The stem and sternpost were the upright hull timbers forming the very bow and stern of the vessel, respectively. In general, their construction on western river steamboats was simple. In the *Howard and Company Record Book,* no specifics are given for the construction of the perpendiculars, or "perps," as they were commonly known. The best example of a sternpost was recorded on *Kentucky,* and it was without distinction. Her sternpost was a vertical timber notched into the keel, fastened on the exterior with an iron fish plate. On the interior the sternpost was fastened to the deadwood.

The best example of a stem was recorded on 2Ct243, which had a stem assembly made of the deadwood, stem, and stemson. On most watercraft the deadwood comprises one or more timbers stacked on top of the keel to fill out the narrow part of the hull in either the bow or stern. Based on the information from 2Ct243, this definition is not applicable to the deadwood of western steamboats. 2Ct243's deadwood also served as the keel farther aft, not a typical feature of boat construction. This

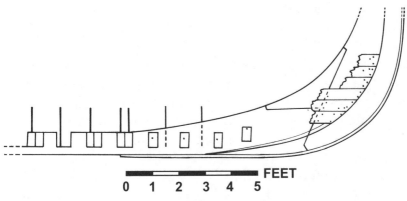

*5.12. The stem of the wreck 3Ct243.*

unusual technique was certainly an adaptation based on the absence of a significant keel. The after portion of the deadwood was notched on its upper face to receive the floors, while farther forward, mortices for cant frames were recorded. The deadwood was scafed to the stem, with a stemson, basically a standing knee, used to reinforce the juncture. An interesting feature of the stems of 2Ct243, *John Walsh,* and *Scotland* was the presence of an iron nosing, a thin band of metal placed along the exterior of the stem to protect it from impacts with ice and driftwood and from general wear and abrasion.

FRAMING

The framing of western river steamboats consisted of flat floors and vertical or nearly vertical futtocks for the run of the hull, with more complex curved frames at the bow and stern. The floors and futtocks were small, generally moulded five to nine inches, and sided three to six inches. The examination of a midship cross-section (see fig. 5.11) indicates a simple framing pattern. A closer examination of the archaeological and historical record, however, demonstrates that the actual framing of a steamboat hull was more complex than any single cross-section can relate.

Along the run of the hull, shipwrights used framing of different sizes, depending on the stresses placed on various parts of the hull. This trend was most notably observed in the remains of *Scotland,* a side-wheeler built in 1855. The moulded dimensions of *Scotland's* floors were consistent throughout the hull, ranging between seven and eight inches. Yet areas of the hull that were subject to excessive stresses were framed with double floors. These were found on average of one for every four floors in the after half of the hull but were more common in the forward half, averaging one out of every three floors. Double floors were especially common in areas that were underneath the engine and boilers.[18]

A pattern of using heavier framing in the forward half of the hull is also reflected in the records of the Howard Ship Yard and Dock Company, whose *Howard and Company Record Book* relates the business of building steamboats, albeit in cryptic form. The following description puts into narrative form the framing pattern to be used on the steamboats *John W. Cannon,* a side-wheeler 252 feet in length built in 1878, and *City of New Orleans,* a 290-foot-long side-wheeler built in 1881. In framing *John W. Cannon,* the floors were 9 inches moulded in the forward part of the hull and 8¼ inches in the after part. The floors were 4½ inches sided for about the first twenty-five frames, then 4 inches sided until about sixteen frames forward of the sternpost; the remaining floors were sided 3½ inches. The spacing between floors was specified to increase at the same intervals that the sided dimension of the floors decreased. Thus, the floors were spaced 13, 14, and 15 inches on centers, respectively, and the futtocks were all 3 inches. A similar pattern was used for framing the *City of New Orleans.* Floor timbers were 9 inches moulded, except for the aftermost forty-eight frames, which were 8½ inches. The cant frames in the stern were 3½ inches sided. From these up to the fiftieth floor abaft the stem, the floors were 4 inches sided and, from that point forward, 4½ inches sided. The floors were spaced on centers 13 inches from the stem to frame forty-two; from frame forty-two to ninety-six, 14 inches; from frame ninety-six to the aft hatch, 15 inches; and from there aft, 16 and 17 inches.[19] Both the archaeological and historical data on framing patterns reinforce the understanding that steamboat hulls were built as lightly as possible. Howard's specifications, which determine scantling sizes down to the half-inch, underscore the value of cutting down the amount of timber used in the hull whenever possible. Overall, the data suggest that framing on western river steamboats was heavier in the forward half of the vessel than in the after half, primarily to support the weight of the machinery.

Among the archaeological examples available for this study, the shape of each frame along the run of the hull indicates that at least three different framing systems were used to build steamboat hulls. These types, based on construction at the turn of the bilge, are standard chine, chine log, and rounded knuckle.

Standard-chine construction appears to be the most common type found on western steamboats, evident in the hulls of *A. S. Ruthven, Scotland, J. D. Hinde, Bertrand,* and 3Ct243. The floors in this type of framing were dead flat across the breadth of the hull, while the futtocks were vertical or near vertical. The intersection of these created a sharp chine at the turn of the bilge. Based on the current data set, three subdivisions of standard chine can be defined. In the cocked-hat technique, a triangular-shaped timber, known as a cocked hat, was used to join the floor and the futtock. The cocked hats of different frames were joined to each other by a longitudinally oriented bilge keelson. The second technique, the futtock chine, was similar to the cocked-hat chine except that, rather than a triangular timber, a piece of compass wood was used to join the floor to the futtock. This juncture was strengthened by the same longitudinally oriented bilge keelson. The use of compass

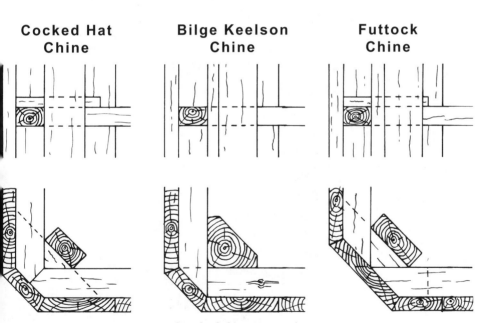

**Cocked Hat Chine**  **Bilge Keelson Chine**  **Futtock Chine**

5.13. *Standard-chine construction.*

wood at the chine, at least for the Howard Ship Yard and Dock Company, seems to have been standard practice. In 1904 John C. Howard wrote, "the Insurance Company required us to use the natural turn of the wood, which we could only get in the roots, for the turn of the knuckle and other places, and root knees were used everywhere."[20] He goes on to relate the tendency for these "root knees" to rot and how that led to an early death for many steamboats. The final standard-chine subdivision is the bilge-keelson chine. In this technique the futtock and floor were fastened to each other at their extremity, and no additional framing timber was used to join the two. The joint between the futtock and floor was reinforced by the bilge keelson.

The second framing method, chine-log construction, has been found in *Cremona* (1852). Given the small data set, it is impossible to know if that vessel's construction represents chine log as a more common tech-

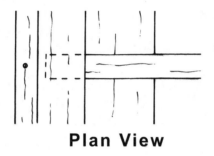

**Plan View**

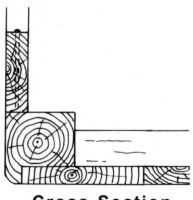

**Cross-Section**

*5.14. Chine-log construction.*

nique or if it was merely an anomaly. *Cremona* is particularly interesting not only because it differs from any other steamboat yet found but also because of its stylistic similarity to the construction of timber-sided scow barges. Her hull was flat bottomed, with vertical sides joined by a chine log. The ends of her floors were morticed into the chine log via a wedged dovetail joint. The futtocks were secured by a mortice in the chine log and a notch cut out of the first side strake. This steamboat's planking was edge fastened, another construction technique unique to *Cremona*, though widely used in building barges. Edge-fastened planking was constructed by affixing thick planks together with iron drift bolts driven vertically down through the upper face of the plank, which effectively welds the side strakes together to form a wall of timber.

The final framing technique, rounded-knuckle construction, has been noted on two vessels, *Arabia* and *Black Cloud*. These vessels, both side-wheelers, had flat bottoms and vertical sides, but they were joined by a rounded transition from one to the other. Rounded-knuckle construction was more labor-intensive than either standard chine or chine log. Compass timber was required for futtocks spanning the turn of the bilge. It was interesting to note that while only two examples of this technique have been found, two of the most detailed contemporary cross-sections of western river steamboats, Thomas Tredgold's depiction of *Buckeye State* (1850) (see fig. 5.6) and Norman S. Russell's drawing of *Memphis* (1860) (see fig. 5.11), show this technique. In his description Russell alludes to the use of rounded-knuckle construction for larger vessels, while "for the smaller class of boats, . . . single frames are used with a knee to scarph [*sic*] the sides and the floors." Russell's description indicates that rounded-knuckle construction would be found in large vessels, while smaller ones would be chine built. The use of rounded knuckle was noted for the building of the steamer *City of Greenville* in 1878 by the Howard Ship Yard. In the specifications for her construction, the 285-foot-long side-wheeler was intended to have "futtocks all 3½ inches [with] Round Knuckle[s]."[21] Future archaeological studies will reveal if the theory of larger vessels having rounded-knuckle construction and smaller steamboats being chine built is generally accurate. The documentation of standard-chine construction on *Scotland*, a 230-foot-long side-wheeler, casts some doubt on this general rule, though *Scotland* may simply be an anomaly.

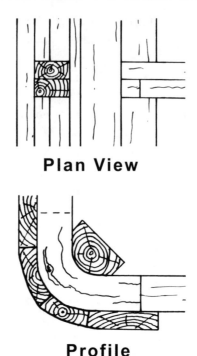

**Plan View**

**Profile**

*5.15. Rounded-knuckle construction.*

Framing in the bow and stern was more complicated than framing in the run of the hull, due to the curvatures in these parts. Room and space at the bow was often decreased relative to the rest of the hull, with the understanding that a strongly framed bow could withstand impact from driftwood and ice. The opposite seems to be the case for the stern. In terms of framing techniques, both cant and half frames were used in the bow and stern. Half frames were those running perpendicular to the keel and divided into two identical, but opposite, sections. Each half frame was fastened to the deadwood. Cant frames were similar to half frames except that they run at varying angles from the keel.[22] These were fastened to either the deadwood in the stern or the stemson in the bow.

The stern framing of the side-wheelers *Kentucky* and *Arabia* show a similar pattern. The lines of both vessels' sterns resemble those of *Buckeye State* (see fig. 5.3). Their floors show considerable deadrise that then flared outward, creating a hollow in the lines of the hull. These complicated lines, intended to get clean water to the rudder, required considerable compass wood. Both vessels also have composite frames made up of several smaller pieces of compass wood. There is little doubt that obtaining large pieces of compass wood in such extreme shapes was simply not practical by the mid–nineteenth century.

## KEELSON

After the framing of a steamboat's hull was completed, the next item to be installed was the keelson. This was an internal stringer that ran fore and aft along the vessel's centerline. It was laid on top of the floors and fastened to both the floors and the keel below. Although contemporary cross-sections of western steamboats tend to portray the keelson as a simple rectangular timber, those documented archaeologically show more variety in their construction. Keelsons can be divided into two categories: keelsons and keelson assemblies. Three vessels in this survey, *Cremona*, *Black Cloud*, and 3Ct243, had keelsons composed of only one timber. Keelson assemblies were present on three vessels, *Kentucky*, *A. S. Ruthven*, and *Bertrand*. *J. D. Hinde* apparently had no keelson.

On most watercraft the keelson served as a longitudinal stiffener,

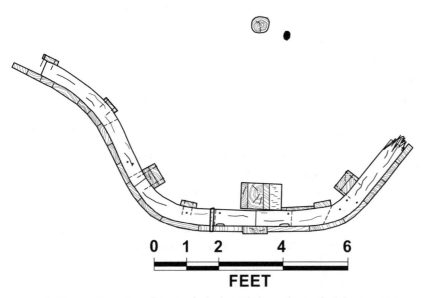

0 1 2 4 6
**FEET**

*5.16. Cross-section view of* Kentucky*'s eleventh frame forward of the sternpost.*

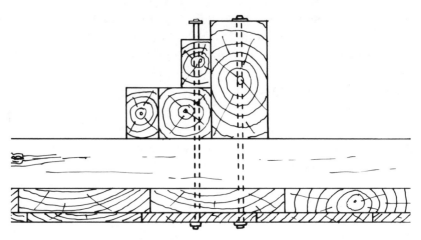

*5.17. Detail of* A. S. Ruthven's *keelson.*

but on western steamboats this seems to have been only a secondary purpose. More importantly, it served as a platform for other features. Longitudinal bulkheads running the length of the vessel were typically mounted on top of the keelson, while this face of the keelson was also commonly notched to receive stanchions supporting the deck above. Braces used to support hog and cross chains were also stepped into the keelson.

### STREAKS, STRINGERS, AND CLAMPS

In addition to the keelson, the steamboat hull had three other longitudinal features: streaks, bilge keelsons, and shelf clamps. The most numerous of these were streaks, of which there were commonly six to twelve per vessel.[23] There were three types of streaks: hold, stanchion, and side. Hold streaks were simple planks that ran fore and aft along the upper faces of the floors. Stanchion streaks were similar to hold streaks except they tended to be larger and formed a step for either stanchions or a bulkhead. Side streaks were fastened to the futtocks along the side of the hull. Streaks were generally moulded two to six inches and sided four to eight inches. All of them strengthened the frames by firmly holding them in a fore-and-aft line.

Bilge keelsons ran longitudinally along the interior of the hull at the point where the sides of the vessel met the bottom. Aside from the keelson, the bilge keelsons were the largest parts in the hold. Although sometimes made of only one piece of wood, they were frequently constructed of two planks laid on top of each other. They generally ranged from six to ten inches thick and from ten to fifteen inches wide. Bilge keelsons served two important purposes. First, they reinforced the juncture between the bottom of the hull and the sides. This was a weak point in the structure, the strength of which was increased by the fore-and-aft nature of the bilge keelson. Second, the knuckle chains, which pulled up on the bilges of the boat, were fastened into them.

The last fore-and-aft feature of note in the steamboat hull were the shelf clamps, planks that ran along the side of the hull and were used to support the deck beams above. These also gave longitudinal strength to the hull.[24] In most sailing vessels the juncture between the deck beam and the side of the hull was braced with a hanging knee. This naturally grown crook served to unite the side of the vessel with the deck. None of the archaeological or historical data indicate that this feature was used on steamboats of this era. At the intersection between the deck beams and the shelf clamp, these pieces were often morticed to receive each other.

PLANKING

The exterior of the hull was sheathed with planking. All of the steamboats examined in this study were caravel built; that is, they were planked so that the seams were smooth, rather than overlapping, as in clinker built. Planking was light, with thickness ranging from $1\frac{1}{4}$ to $3\frac{1}{2}$ inches. One vessel, *A. S. Ruthven,* showed an unusual planking feature. Her hull's exterior was sheathed with a one-inch-thick layer of sacrificial planking. This shielded the standard planking from abrasion and damage caused by frequent groundings and encounters with driftwood. This is the only known example of a western river steamboat with this protective feature. Planking at the steamboat's bow, which was constantly impacted by driftwood and ice during the winter, was often sheathed with sheet iron. This has been archaeologically documented on 3Ct243, *Bertrand,* and *John Walsh.*

Wales were used on some vessels too. A wale, in essence a thick strake of planking, was traditionally used to bind together and strengthen the hull. It is unlikely that wales on western steamboats performed this function. Instead, they were designed to fend off driftwood and ice. When present, they comprised the first and second planking strake. This location, at the approximate load waterline for most steamboats, would put it in contact with the most flotsam. A wale one inch thicker than the adjacent planking was found on the Clatterwheel Wreck.[25] Tredgold's cross-section of *Buckeye State* also shows a wale (see fig. 5.6).

BULKHEADS

One universal attribute of the western-river-steamboat hull was the use of longitudinal bulkheads. These components helped prevent hogging by creating a wall, arch, or latticework of interlocking timbers that spanned the distance from the bottom of the hull to the underside of the deck beams and ran the vessel's entire length. At a minimum, steamboats had one bulkhead down the centerline, but three or more bulkheads evenly spaced in the hull were common. Their bases rested on either the keelson, if the bulkhead ran along the centerline, or on a stanchion streak, if it was located off to the side. The tops were fastened to overhead stanchion streaks, which were in turn fastened to the deck beams. Three types of bulkheads have been found either in the archaeological or historical record: solid, diagonal bracing, and arched.

Solid-timber bulkheads were identified in the remains of *J. D. Hinde, Ed. F. Dix,* and *Bertrand; J. D. Hinde* had three, while *Bertrand* and *Ed. F. Dix* were fitted with only one each. The bulkheads on these vessels were composed of two structural members, stanchions and planks. Vertically oriented stanchions were generally positioned at intervals of two to four feet and were typically located underneath deck beams. Stanchion bases were morticed and/or fastened into the keelson or stanchion streak; the tops were similarly attached to an overhead stanchion streak. A wall of thin planking was nailed to them so that a solid wall of timber ran down the entire length of the vessel.

Diagonal bracing was a method commonly used to prevent hogging on oceangoing ships in the mid–nineteenth century. The earliest use of this technique is unknown, but it was described in the *Journal of the Franklin Institute* for use on naval vessels in 1846, and this article notes that construction using that method had been employed since 1835. The advantages of diagonal trussing are described in contemporary shipbuilding

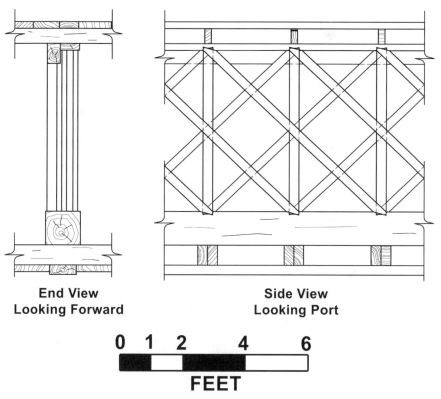

**End View**
**Looking Forward**

**Side View**
**Looking Port**

0   1   2       4       6

**FEET**

*5.18. These cross-sections of* Kentucky's *hull display
the arrangement of her diagonal bracing.*

literature. Andrew Murray and Robert Murray state that inserting a diagonal of "a fixed or unalterable length into any piece of framework will
tend to prevent alteration of form, . . . [because] the duty required of
the two diagonals in resisting any change was different, the one being
required to resist extension, and the other to resist compression."[26]

Diagonal bracing was recorded on *Kentucky* and *John Walsh*. Each set of
*Kentucky*'s diagonal bracing was built of three timbers, two diagonally oriented and one vertical. At their intersection they were joined by a single
iron fastener. The tops of the bracing were morticed into the stanchion
streak, the bottoms into the keelson. Each set of three bracing timbers
overlapped the set forward and aft, helping unite the whole structure.

{ 109 }

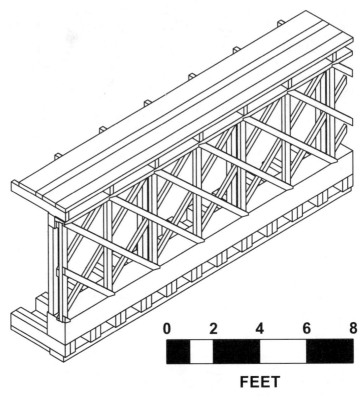

*5.19. An isometric drawing of the arrangement of* Kentucky*'s diagonal bracing.*

The latticework was further tied together by vertical iron tie rods that extended from the stanchion streak to the keel. *John Walsh*'s diagonal bracing was similar to *Kentucky*'s, however it lack the vertical timbers. Evenly spaced vertical tie rods also bound together *John Walsh*'s bracing.[27]

Arched bulkheads have not yet been found in an archaeological context, but they are described and illustrated in one primary source. Norman Russell, writing in a technical journal in 1861, notes the use of an arched bulkhead in light-water boats. He describes them as "a series of small hogframes, about 30 feet long, which take the place of the solid bulkhead; a number of posts radiate from the kelson, and over their tops, three 2-inch planks are bent like an arch, and fastened down at their end to the kelson; the space between being as before filled in, completes an extremely light and strong bulkhead."[28]

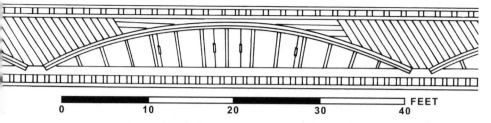

5.20. *Detail showing an arched bulkhead.*

### GUARDS, DECKING, AND DECK BEAMS

The shallow hull of the western river steamboat limited the storage area in the hold. Consequently, most of the cargo was carried on the main deck, requiring that this area be expanded as much as possible. The deck's cargo capacity was significantly increased by the overhanging guards. On side-wheelers, guards typically added 50–75 percent of breadth, depending on the width of the paddle wheels, to the main deck relative to that of the hull. As the length of paddle-wheel buckets progressively increased throughout the period, so did the width of the guards. On stern-wheelers, the guards were generally much smaller, but the hull was proportionately beamier.[29]

Decking is rarely preserved on shipwrecks, but due to the tendency of the rivers in the Mississippi Basin to quickly bury hull remains, excellent preservation is common for steamboat hulls. Ten of the seventeen investigated vessels had portions of the decking, deck beams, or guards preserved. In general, the construction of these members was simple. Deck beams ran across the breadth of the hull; near the gunwale, they were lap joined to outrigger beams. Having a slight bit of camber, the beams allowed the deck to shed water and increased headroom in the hold. The outrigger beams extended out past the lines of the hull, forming the base of the guards. The decking, made up of boards 1–1½ inches thick, was fastened to these beams. Bulkheads, stanchions, and the shelf clamps supported the deck beams from below. At the outboard edge of the hull, where the deck and outrigger beams exited the lines of the hull, the futtock heads were often cut out to make way for them, and the shelf clamp and planking were notched to help secure them. A variation of this athwartship pattern was used for the sterns of side-wheelers, which often had deck beams that formed a radial pattern, allowing the guard to be extended aft of the transom.

The dimensions of deck beams varied according to the weight they supported. Deck beams were larger in areas underneath machinery or where hatches were present. Outrigger beams were similarly varied, although larger ones tended to be placed underneath the cookhouse, at the ends of the paddle-wheel housing, and where cross chains tied in to support the guards. The pattern of deck- and outrigger-beam size was recorded by the Howard Ship Yard in the specifications for the construction of the *John W. Cannon* (1878). For this side-wheeler, the deck beams, unless otherwise stated, were 7 inches moulded. Most were 3½–4 inches sided, though the first fifteen deck beams were 6 and 7 inches sided and the hatch and doctor beams were 4¼ inches sided. Boiler beams were 11 inches sided and 14 inches moulded, made up of one solid timber. Those supporting the paddle wheel and cylinder timbers were 11 inches sided along the centerline, 12 inches sided at the gunwale, and 9 inches sided at the outboard edge of the guards. The fantail beams were 5 inches sided. Outrigger beams were 10¼ inches moulded at the gunwale and 7 inches moulded at the outboard edge; the sided dimension depended on their location. Most outrigger beams were 3½ or 4 inches sided, though any with a cross chain affixed was 6 inches sided, and the two under the cookhouse were 4¼ inches sided.[30]

TRUSSING

Between 1835 and 1841, hull distortion caused by the extreme length-to-breadth ratio led to the application of hog chains to vessels' hulls. Archaeological remains of trussing include the chains themselves and the footling as well as the braces used to support the chains.

A footling was a longitudinally oriented wooden structure, positioned on top of the floors, used to hold the foot of a brace and distribute its downward force. The hog chains on side-wheelers were arranged so that most of the footlings were just port or starboard of the centerline, while on stern-wheelers footlings were also found near the bilges to support the braces from the two longitudinal hog chains.

Footlings have been documented on three of the vessels in this survey. *Kentucky*'s footling was used to support its main hog chain. It was located adjacent to and on the starboard side of the keelson; it was seven

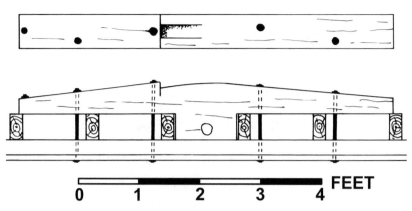

5.21. *Plan view and profile of a footling from* A. S. Ruthven.

feet long, sided 4 inches, and moulded 9¼ inches. The tops of both the
forward and after ends of the footling were rounded, its underside was
notched to fit over the floors, and it had a mortice cut into its inboard
face to receive a brace. The footlings on *A. S. Ruthven* and *Bertrand* were
similar to each other. Both were trapezoidal in shape and notched to receive a brace.

Braces were wooden posts used to support the hog chains. The foot
of the brace was morticed into a footling, while the chain was suspended
over the top. Depending on the location and nature of the brace, it was
oriented vertically or canted forward or aft. Braces for cross chains and
knuckle chains were vertical, while hog-chain braces were canted forward in the forward part of the hull, vertical in the middle, and aft in
the stern. The remains of *Kentucky* contained two preserved braces, one
vertical cross-chain brace and one canted hog-chain brace. One six-by-
six-inch brace, used to support a cross chain, was morticed into the inboard face of both the keelson assembly and a footling. The mortice,
which was divided evenly between these two structural members, was
positioned in that manner to better distribute the downward force of
the brace throughout the hull. The larger of the two braces measured
seven inches square. It rose from the bottom of the hull at a fifty-eight-
degree angle toward the aft end of the vessel; this angle indicated the
brace supported the longitudinal hog chain and allowed more force to
be exerted on itself than if it had been oriented vertically.

In an archaeological context, the types of chains (hog, cross, and

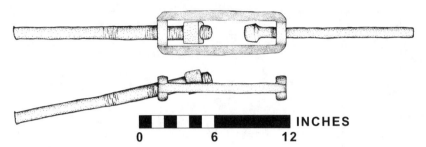

INCHES

0      6      12

5.22. *Drawing of a turnbuckle from one of* Kentucky*'s cross chains.*

knuckle) can be differentiated by their sizes, numbers, and positions. Longitudinal hog chains were larger and less common than either cross or knuckle chains. In order to adjust tension, all chains were fitted with turnbuckles. *Kentucky*'s longitudinal hog chain was two inches in diameter, while its cross chains were one inch. Cross chains are common at steamboat sites, though they are typically out of context. During the working life of the steamboat, they span the distance between the main deck and the boiler deck; however, no archaeological example of a steamboat has been preserved up to the boiler deck, thus the cross chains are in a state of disarray. Knuckle chains are also a common find, but their location in the bottom of the hull allows for better preservation.

Features relating to the trussing of hulls are some of the most common finds at wreckage sites, attesting to their importance in steamboat construction.

### Machinery

Mechanical characteristics of western river steamboats of this period did not fundamentally differ from those built in the early 1830s. By 1835, the high-pressure engine powered by a battery of boilers was both universally adopted and fully developed in the essential points of its construction.

During the 1830s and early 1840s, the trend in steamboat machinery was toward more boilers, with six or even nine eventually common. The disadvantage of the extra weight in iron and water was subsequently realized, and in the following decade the trend was reversed. By 1850, four or five boilers were again typical, with similar diameters, but with an increase in length reaching twenty-eight to thirty feet.[31] Boiler shells in the 1830s were one-fifth to one-sixth of an inch thick, but this increased to one-quarter of an inch by 1850.[32] The use of flues, the tubes allowing the passage of hot gases from the furnace through the boiler, continued during this period. In the years following 1860, the number of flues increased to up to six per boiler, but two was the standard between 1830 and 1860.

Through much of this period, water was still supplied to the boilers using the feed-water pump (described in the preceding chapter). This method was slowly phased out with the advent of a small, independent, steam-driven flywheel pump in the early 1840s. This pump was known as the doctor because of the hope that it would cure all the evils of the steamboat by supplying a steady stream of water to the boilers, thereby preventing explosions. The doctor also worked the bilge pumps and supplied the hose in case of a fire. Although it did reduce the number of boiler explosions, the doctor's effect was lessened because it was not widely used until after 1850, and even then it was not employed on the smallest class of steamboats.[33]

Although the manner in which this device worked is complicated to explain, in reality it was a simple piece of machinery. Its working parts were easily accessible and could be repaired by most engineers. The doctor was on the main deck just aft of the boilers. Its motive power was received via an auxiliary steam line stemming from the boilers. Steam was injected into the vertically oriented steam cylinder, forcing the piston and connecting rod to work. The connecting rod transferred its up-and-down motion to one end of a side lever; another rod connected to the side lever turned the central feature of the doctor, a flywheel. Once

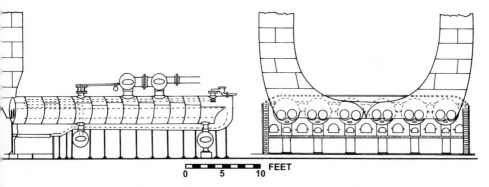

5.23. *The typical boilers of a western river steamboat.*

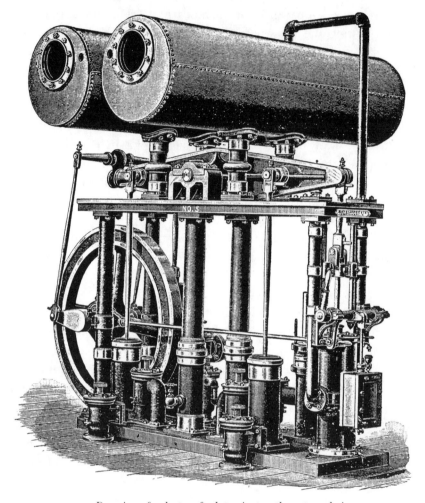

*5.24. Drawing of a doctor of a late-nineteenth-century design.*

in motion, the heavy cast-iron flywheel moderated the speed of the machinery by its weight and inertia. The motion of the side lever additionally worked two sets of pumps, lifting and force pumps. The single-acting cold-water, or lifting, pumps drew water from the river and forced it into the heaters, composed of riveted wrought-iron shells with cast-iron heads. Here the cold water was heated by the engine's exhaust steam as it passed through via a central pipe. The hot-water, or force, pumps took the water from the heater and transferred it into the boilers.[34]

The combustion process powered steamboat machinery, with wood being the typical fuel (though coal was used as well). The ability to regulate the combustion was important: increased fuel consumption translated into higher steam pressures and more power to the engine, while reduced consumption meant less power but a savings in the cost of fuel. In early steamboats air was conveyed to the furnace by natural draft. In the 1840s and 1850s, artificial methods were applied with varying levels of success, but none replaced natural draft; many contemporaries believed this was due to the stubborn nature of western engineers.

One of these techniques employed steam blowers. A small amount of steam was diverted from the steam line that fed the engine and was vented into either the flues or the chimneys, thereby diminishing the specific gravity of the gases around it and aiding the draft of the furnace. The diverted steam was normally built up in a steam box and injected into the flues or chimneys by way of a small pipe with a perforated end. Steam blowers were not widely adopted on the western rivers because many engineers believed they burned out the flues and breeching. The venting into the flues and chimneys also tended to promote corrosion, thus shortening their lifespan. Furthermore, the diversion of steam from the engines resulted in diminished power. Not only did steam blowers need frequent repair, but many engineers believed they burned more fuel and depleted the water supply in the boilers more rapidly.[35]

Fan blowers, another method of creating artificial draft, were also never widely adopted on western rivers, though they did have supporters. A fan making approximately seven hundred revolutions per minute, powered by an auxiliary steam line from the boilers and normally positioned at the aft end of the ash pan, was used to force a flow of air into the furnace. While it worked on the same principle as natural draft, the fan blower could be made much more intense, if desired. This innovation was not without its drawbacks, both real and perceived. Fan blowers were costly, heavy, and large and required frequent repair. Some engineers complained that the blowers were loud and the increased airflow forced more sparks and soot up the chimneys.[36] The machines also took power away from the engines, thereby slowing the vessel. Finally, they concentrated the heat of the fire on the grate bars, causing them to burn out.

For several reasons, neither steam nor fan blowers ever entirely superceded natural draft. Most important of these reasons was the strong prejudice of the engineers against using any type of new technology. By the 1840s, both the engines and boilers of western steamboats were well established, and most engineers were reluctant to radically alter a device that already performed its duty well. Furthermore, steamboat machinery had been made as cheap, light, and simple as possible. Introducing a complicated, expensive device to do a task that was already performed at no cost was not acceptable to most engineers.

Consistent with most other features of the steamboat, the dimensions of the chimneys increased throughout this period. By 1850, chimneys commonly rose at least forty-five feet above the boilers, and on larger vessels eighty feet was not unusual. Their diameter also increased, with typical measurements being between forty-two and sixty inches. To construct a chimney, its diameter was calculated by determining the aggregate sectional area of the boiler flues and multiplying that number by either 2.5 or 3. That number divided by two would be the sectional area for each chimney.[37]

The last significant development in the construction of chimneys occurred in the mid-1830s with the addition of hinges. Made of cast iron, they allowed the upper portion of the chimney to be lowered. This feature was a direct response to the increasing number of relatively low bridges across western rivers, especially the Ohio; building bridges high enough to allow steamboat traffic to pass beneath them during periods of high water proved impractical. Chimneys designed to be lowered were built stronger than those intended to be static, using thicker sheet iron for the skin and vertically oriented iron bars running along the inside for reinforcement.[38]

The engine of the western river steamboat was not an awe-inspiring sight; it had little if any bright work and generally lacked the refinement that was common in other types of steamboat engines.[39] Despite its plain appearance, it was a light, powerful, inexpensive, and easily maintained machine, well adapted to the function it served.

Early western steamboats had one engine, but after 1840 many larger packets were equipped with two, each working its own paddle wheel.[40] Two steam engines provided more power, but the primary advantage was the maneuverability they provided. The ability to stop or back one paddle wheel while keeping the other going forward was essential in the navigation of narrow, winding rivers. Each engine was located near the edge of the hull, thereby leaving open space for cargo between them. Steam pressure slowly increased through the years, and by 1850, pressures of between 130 and 160 pounds per square inch were typical for packets on the Ohio River.[41]

A steam engine rested on a pair of heavy timber frames, known as the cylinder timbers. The timbers rested on either the main deck or the floors in the bottom of the hull. They spanned many deck beams or floors, thereby spreading the weight of the engine across a large area of the hull. The outboard cylinder timber was known as the main timber, and the interior as the auxiliary timber. The engine cylinder and cross-head guides rested on the forward portion of the cylinder timbers. Continuing aft, they were angled upward, meeting the paddle-wheel shaft, but only the main cylinder timber was extended aft to carry the shaft. Both the historical and archaeological record indicate that cylinder timbers were not necessarily made of a solid wall of wood. Depictions of *Buckeye State*'s engine and the cross-section of *Memphis* show cylinder timbers with gaps in them. These gaps, sometimes braced with angled beams, were intended to lessen the weight of the cylinder timbers. This feature was also recorded archaeologically on *Homer*.[42]

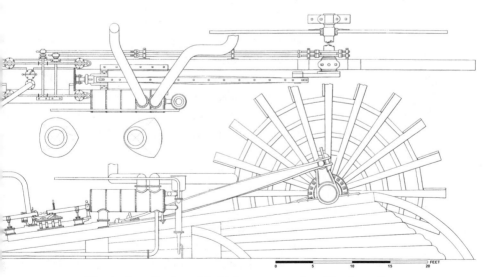

5.25. *Plan and profile view of the high-pressure engine of* Buckeye State.

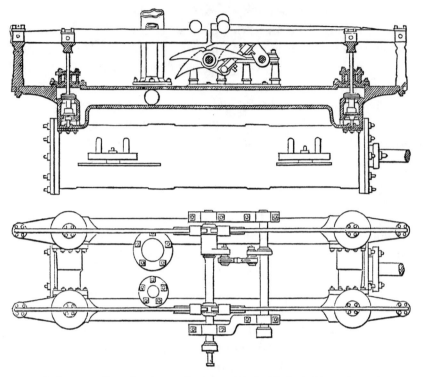

5.26. *A cross-section of a steam cylinder equipped with the poppet-valve system.*

The heart of the steam engine was its cylinder. The cylinder was oriented just above horizontal at an angle sufficient to intersect the center of the paddle-wheel shaft. Cylinder size increased considerably in the early years of steamboating, with the average diameter of twenty inches in 1827 increasing to twenty-eight inches by 1838. After 1840, cylinder diameters stabilized due primarily to the trend toward using two engines.[43]

Admission and exhaust of steam in to and out of the cylinder was effected in four valve chests and regulated by the poppet-valve system.[44] In this system the cylinder was cast with two nozzles at each end, each having a valve chamber. There was therefore one chamber at either end for the admission of fresh steam and one at either end for the exhaustion of spent steam. During each stroke of the piston, steam was admitted to one end of the cylinder and simultaneously exhausted from the other. The admitted steam was then cut off at some point in the stroke and allowed to expand for the remainder. This process then repeated itself from the opposite end to complete a cycle.[45]

The timing of the poppet valves was governed by two cams on the paddle-wheel shaft. These cams, oblong discs mounted on the shaft, created an oscillating motion when the paddle-wheel shaft turned. This oscillation was transformed into a fore-and-aft motion by an iron frame, or yoke, within which the cams were contained. The yoke in turn was welded to a long, wrought-iron bar called the rock shaft. The end of the rock shaft ended at a point near the middle of the engine cylinder. Here it was fitted with a double wiper, the alternating motion of which lifted the levers and opened or closed the valves on the cylinder.[46] Thus the rotary motion of the paddle wheel caused the cam to oscillate, giving a reciprocal motion to the yoke and rock shaft, and finally causing the wipers to either lift or let fall the valves on the cylinder.

Regulating the power applied to the engine was as simple as managing how much steam was injected into the cylinder. This could be manually controlled by inserting a two-and-one-half-inch-square billet of wood, called the club, between the rocker arm and the lever that lifted the inlet valve. Inserting the club at the proper time provided additional steam to the cylinder and, therefore, extra energy to the paddle wheel. Alternately, the full-stroke cam could be employed. This device allowed live steam to be fed into the cylinder for the entire length of its stroke.

5.27. Profile of a full-stroke cam and yoke.

The full-stroke cam was used at times when maximum power was needed, such as starting from a complete stop or ascending rapids. Under normal operating conditions, the one-half-, five-eighth-, or three-quarter-stroke cam was employed. These cut off the steam at various positions within the stroke and allowed the steam to push the cylinder by expansion through the remainder.[47] The use of the cut-off cam, as these latter types were known, resulted in considerable fuel savings.

The reciprocal motion of the piston was turned into the rotary motion of the paddle wheel through a series of simple devices. One end of the piston rod was welded to the piston; the other end had a U-shaped bracket affixed to it. This bracket, known as the crosshead, was fitted with a wrist pin. This wrist pin was punched through the end of the connecting rod, known on western steamboats as the pitman, thus allowing it to pivot on the rod's axis.[48] (The construction of the pitman was unique to western rivers; it was composed of a wooden timber, most commonly pine, tapered at each end with two wrought-iron straps bolted around the edges.)[49] The aft end of the pitman connected to the crank on the paddle-wheel shaft. In practice, steam was injected into the cylinder, forcing the piston inside the cylinder to move. As steam pushed the piston, the piston rod was also forced to move. The movement of the piston rod was transferred to the pitman via the wrist pin. The aft end of the pitman was connected to the crank on the paddle-wheel shaft, which was compelled to move in a circular fashion by the pitman. As the pitman rotated the crank, the paddle wheel turned.

Upon completion of each stroke of the piston, steam was exhausted through a metal cylinder, known as the coughing box or feed-water heater, used for heating the water before it was fed to the boilers. This interesting device was a cylindrical shell of either rolled iron or copper enclosed at both ends. It was laid on its side, allowing exhausted steam from the cylinder to enter at its underside and cold river water at its topside. The interior contained a series of iron or copper plates oriented horizontally and separated from each other by three to five inches of open space. These plates spanned the entire length of the heater, and alternating ends of the plates had holes cut into them. The effect of this system was such that water was sent into the top and forced to descend along all of the iron plates in a lateral back-and-forth fashion until it reached the bottom. While the water cascaded down through the levels, steam was forced upward, thus imparting its heat to the water. Upon reaching the bottom of the heater, the water was fed via the feed-water pump, or doctor, to the boilers.[50]

Often during this process, all of the steam would be condensed; if it was not, it could still be put to use. Excess steam could be piped into the paddle-wheel boxes to prevent ice from forming on the paddle wheels or into the chimney to aid the draft of the boilers. It might also be allowed to escape out through a small chimney past the hurricane deck.[51]

Paddle wheels grew in nearly every dimension during this period. Ruben Miller, a steamboat builder and owner, estimated that in 1840 the average diameter of steamboat paddle wheels was eighteen to twenty-two feet; only ten years later, the average was twenty-five to thirty-one feet. Additionally, the width and depth of the buckets increased, though not in proportion to the diameter.[52]

The center of a paddle wheel was the paddle-wheel shaft, an iron rod to which the rest of the wheel was attached. The shaft rested upon the cylinder timbers inside the lines of the hull and the guard timber at the outboard edge of the guard. Upon each of these beams it was held in place with a cast-iron pillow block. The shaft was rotated by the crank, which was rotated by the pitman and engine. The outboard end of the shaft had two or three faceted areas to which the flanges were attached. The flanges formed the central portion of the paddle wheel from which the arms radiated outward. The outer circumference of a flange contained pockets into which the arms were secured. The arms were hewn to fit snugly in these pockets and to expand for an even tighter fit when

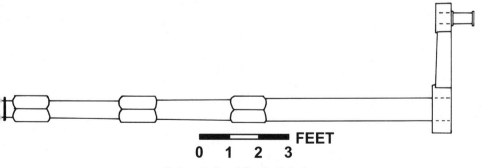

**FEET**
0  1  2  3

5.28. A typical paddle-wheel shaft.

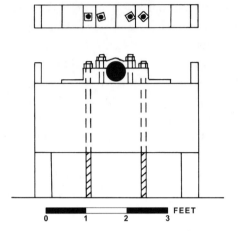

5.29. *A typical pillow block.*

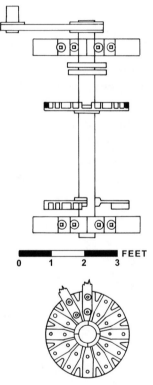

5.30. *A typical paddle-wheel flange.*

wet. Spacing between the arms was maintained by several devices. The most important of these was a pair of wrought-iron circular bands bolted to the arms. Each was fastened to either the interior or exterior face of the arms. The gaps between the bands were filled with wooden blocks, locked in place by keys driven into the space between the arm and the block. This iron-and-wood circle was paralleled by one or more rows of wooden blocking. The arms were also locked into place by small wedges of wood, known as cocked hats, fastened between the arms just outside the flanges. The final features of the paddle wheel were its buckets, which provided resistance in the water, which in turn drove the vessel. These were simple planks of wood bolted to the arms, with a batten used to keep the bolt from pulling through the bucket.[53] Buckets were frequently damaged, so several spares were carried onboard at all times.

# CONCLUSIONS

Between 1811 and 1860, the trans-Appalachian West underwent a fundamental transformation. At the beginning of the nineteenth century, as far as Europeans and Euro-Americans were concerned, the West, although it showed potential, was an immense wilderness having little substantive economic import or consequence. By 1830, however, steam technology in the form of the western river steamboat had entirely changed the regional landscape and character.

In the early years of American nationhood, a trickle of settlers made their way into the lands west of the Appalachian Mountains. It was a region inhabited mostly by Native Americans, with a few rough backwoodsmen and hardscrabble farmers carving out an existence in a region entirely removed from European refinement. Residents realized early the value of the Mississippi Basin's rivers. Two general types of vernacular craft, flatboats and keelboats, were developed to transport the region's agricultural products downriver to New Orleans, where their cargos were transshipped to markets around the world. These vessels were adequate for downstream travel, but the upstream journey was much more difficult. The simple flatboat, with its boxlike hull, was sold for lumber upon arriving in New Orleans, while the diminutive keelboat was packed full of trade goods for the over-two-thousand-mile grueling upstream journey. This was a hindrance to the West's ability to import the items its citizens demanded; the problem lay not in supply, but in transportation. The difficulties of importing trade goods directly affected the downstream flow of commodities. Without a corresponding influx of manufactured articles, the export of goods and the development of the region in general were hampered.

The first steamboat was introduced to the western waters in 1811 by

Robert Fulton, but neither this vessel nor those of the following decade had any significant economic effect on the region. The early steamboats were propelled by a wide array of engine types set within deep hulls; their machinery and hull type were unsuited to the shallow and swift western rivers. They often had features such as sails, bowsprits, below-deck cabins, and figureheads, vestiges of oceangoing vessels soon recognized as useless and subsequently discarded.

In the 1820s and 1830s, the steamboat was rapidly adapted to western river conditions through a process of trial and error by regional ship-wrights and steam-engine builders. These craftsmen pragmatically undertook the job of creating a vessel type that could successfully travel the swift and shallow rivers. Steamboat hulls became increasingly shallow, longer, and more flat bottomed. Lack of space in the hold dictated the use of decks above the waterline. The powerful, inexpensive, wasteful, and lightweight high-pressure steam engine was universally adopted as the power plant of choice. The number of trees consumed by the inefficient engine was equaled only by those required to build the short-lived steamboat hulls. In a region where timber, coal, and iron were plentiful, the conservation of natural resources was never a limiting factor in the construction and operation of steamboats; in fact, these regional attributes helped dictate the vessel type's form and machinery.

The consequences of the steamboat were numerous, affecting society at all levels. These must be viewed in relation to the social and economic upheaval engulfing the country at the time. Known by historians as the market revolution, this process changed the American societal framework from one of subsistence farming to market-oriented agriculture, which suddenly had the potential to create wealth. The market revolution created outlets for producers to sell their excess goods, but new transportation systems were necessary to provide access to markets for the majority of the population. The resulting advancements are collectively known as the transportation revolution and include better roads, canals, steamboats, locomotives, and bridges. All of these contributed to the economic integration of the United States, especially in the states east of the Appalachian Mountains. The West, however, presented a more challenging set of problems when it came to improving transportation. The region itself was geographically enormous, sparsely settled, and densely wooded. These characteristics did not lend themselves to intensive and often expensive building projects such as canals, rail-roads, roads, and bridges. The steamboat was an ideal technology, how-ever, because it worked on an existing pathway: the trans-Appalachian West's extensive navigable river system. Not only did the steamboat con-veniently take advantage of an existing natural network, but they were also much less costly and labor intensive to build and operate, and more efficient, than other modes of transportation.

What the steamboat did require, however, was a structure adapted to the conditions on western rivers. The hulls became entirely flat bot-tomed, with multiple decks rising high above the waterline. In the late 1830s or early 1840s, hog chains were first applied to steamboats. These devices prevented the hull from hogging, or sagging, thereby allowing shipwrights to build vessels with lighter materials. This reduced the weight of the vessel and the amount of water it drew while allowing the cargo capacity to increase significantly. The steamboat's ability to carry massive amounts of freight facilitated its use in the transportation of cotton, which became one of the most profitable sectors of the Ameri-can economy through the Civil War; the steamboat was a crucial link in its transportation and trade. By the 1840s and 1850s, the great major-ity of the West's commerce was carried by river steamboats.

These vessels now are gone from the western rivers, but the water-logged hulks of those lost in service likely number in the hundreds, if not more. Archaeological studies have been conducted on seventeen such wrecks. The construction features of these vessels tend to be well preserved because of the rivers' predisposition to meander. Overall, these studies confirm what was already known from the historic record: steamboat hulls were long, narrow, flat, and lightly built. With that over-riding pattern in mind, many features of western-river-steamboat con-struction are becoming much better understood through the archaeo-logical record. Data from excavations have shown that the techniques and knowledge that western shipwrights used to build steamboats re-sulted in a surprisingly complex vessel type. Every feature was in some way affected by the conditions of the western rivers. The lines of each steamboat were dictated by the trade route and purpose for which that vessel was intended. Those that transported primarily passengers tended to have sharp lines in the bow, while freight and low-water boats tended to have full lines in the bow. The framing of steamboat hulls also belies a complicated construction strategy. Larger-dimension timbers were used in areas of the hull that were under greater stress. In other areas the smallest-dimension timber that could adequately meet the physical requirements was used. The light construction of the hull was greatly advanced with the application of hog, cross, and knuckle chains. The western river steamboat was a marvel of engineering.

This study has sought to build the groundwork for further archaeological investigation of western river steamboats by meshing the historical record with known archaeological data. Many gaps in our understanding of steamboat construction and machinery stem from the limited number of archaeologically excavated vessels and the absence of any archaeological data on the years before 1830. The potential information to be gained from steamboat-wreckage sites is not, however, limited to the details of ship construction. Based on the two vessels that have been entirely excavated, *Arabia* and *Bertrand,* it is plausible to argue that the Mississippi Basin's steamboat wrecks contain the nation's largest collection of intact nineteenth-century material culture. Details about passengers and cargo and information on broader topics, such as western expansion, socioeconomic trends, and gender and ethnic issues, can all conceivably be gleaned from steamboat wrecks. Certainly, future archaeological studies will uncover much that we do not currently know.

# APPENDIX 1
# WESTERN RIVER STEAMBOAT CONSTRUCTION AND TONNAGE, 1811-80

*Source:* Prudy, *Report on Steam Navigation in the United States,* pp. 13–14.

| PITTSBURGH | | | CINCINNATI | | | LOUISVILLE | | | WESTERN RIVERS | | |
|---|---|---|---|---|---|---|---|---|---|---|---|
| year | no. | tonnage | year | no. | tonnage | year | no. | tonnage | year | no. | tonnage |
| 1811 | 1 | 100.00 | 1811 | 0 | 0 | 1811 | 0 | 0 | 1811 | 1 | 100.00 |
| 1812 | 0 | 0 | 1812 | 0 | 0 | 1812 | 0 | 0 | 1812 | 0 | 0 |
| 1813 | 1 | 25.00 | 1813 | 0 | 0 | 1813 | 0 | 0 | 1813 | 1 | 25.00 |
| 1814 | 2 | 385.67 | 1814 | 0 | 0 | 1814 | 0 | 0 | 1814 | 2 | 385.07 |
| 1815 | 4 | 965.71 | 1815 | 0 | 0 | 1815 | 1 | 112.00 | 1815 | 5 | 1,077.85 |
| 1816 | 1 | 131.80 | 1816 | 0 | 0 | 1816 | 0 | 0 | 1816 | 4 | 859.23 |
| 1817 | 2 | 338.80 | 1817 | 1 | 203.01 | 1817 | 1 | 106.25 | 1817 | 5 | 702.52 |
| 1818 | 5 | 1,226.48 | 1818 | 4 | 523.29 | 1818 | 4 | 1,106.46 | 1818 | 15 | 3,099.38 |
| 1819 | 2 | 501.71 | 1819 | 6 | 1,551.01 | 1819 | 12 | 2,375.93 | 1819 | 23 | 5,315.66 |
| 1820 | 3 | 298.75 | 1820 | 1 | 150.00 | 1820 | 6 | 1,309.65 | 1820 | 15 | 2,642.52 |
| 1821 | 1 | 263.59 | 1821 | 1 | 236.60 | 1821 | 0 | 0 | 1821 | 3 | 545.72 |
| 1822 | 1 | 120.90 | 1822 | 3 | 277.50 | 1822 | 2 | 204.04 | 1822 | 11 | 1,013.42 |
| 1823 | 5 | 715.76 | 1823 | 4 | 538.39 | 1823 | 4 | 375.17 | 1823 | 17 | 2,278.28 |
| 1824 | 6 | 1,135.28 | 1824 | 9 | 1,593.77 | 1824 | 5 | 442.76 | 1824 | 20 | 3,171.81 |
| 1825 | 3 | 364.67 | 1825 | 10 | 2,085.37 | 1825 | 5 | 615.75 | 1825 | 18 | 3,065.79 |
| 1826 | 12 | 2,649.09 | 1826 | 13 | 2,148.67 | 1826 | 10 | 1,766.00 | 1826 | 35 | 6,563.76 |
| 1827 | 12 | 2,072.58 | 1827 | 15 | 2,387.10 | 1827 | 6 | 784.93 | 1827 | 33 | 5,244.61 |
| 1828 | 11 | 1,541.42 | 1828 | 5 | 1,186.51 | 1828 | 2 | 250.34 | 1828 | 19 | 3,043.05 |
| 1829 | 18 | 3,577.36 | 1829 | 17 | 3,833.81 | 1829 | 1 | 150.36 | 1829 | 36 | 7,561.53 |
| 1830 | 15 | 1,934.17 | 1830 | 11 | 1,714.80 | 1830 | 7 | 1,162.18 | 1830 | 33 | 4,811.15 |
| 1831 | 15 | 2,055.91 | 1831 | 10 | 1,752.61 | 1831 | 2 | 195.23 | 1831 | 27 | 4,003.75 |
| 1832 | 41 | 6,073.17 | 1832 | 35 | 4,340.87 | 1832 | 9 | 1,498.20 | 1832 | 86 | 12,187.43 |
| 1833 | 24 | 3,193.09 | 1833 | 19 | 2,182.70 | 1833 | 8 | 921.47 | 1833 | 44 | 5,548.32 |
| 1834 | 30 | 4,220.10 | 1834 | 25 | 2,459.45 | 1834 | 9 | 1,327.62 | 1834 | 62 | 8,263.31 |
| 1835 | 32 | 3,384.14 | 1835 | 8 | 1,079.05 | 1835 | 8 | 1,546.90 | 1835 | 51 | 5,718.35 |
| 1836 | 68 | 8,386.41 | 1836 | 29 | 4,191.85 | 1836 | 9 | 1,714.00 | 1836 | 107 | 14,478.85 |
| 1837 | 66 | 10,736.40 | 1837 | 38 | 8,264.16 | 1837 | 8 | 1,389.90 | 1837 | 113 | 21,500.09 |
| 1838 | 43 | 7,424.83 | 1838 | 9 | 1,456.42 | 1838 | 7 | 1,332.88 | 1838 | 66 | 12,626.27 |
| 1839 | 46 | 5,387.86 | 1839 | 38 | 4,863.83 | 1839 | 11 | 2,101.50 | 1839 | 108 | 14,454.61 |
| 1840 | 21 | 2,407.18 | 1840 | 22 | 3,042.52 | 1840 | 5 | 1,090.53 | 1840 | 63 | 9,223.86 |
| 1841 | 34 | 4,983.41 | 1841 | 32 | 5,585.82 | 1841 | 19 | 4,416.77 | 1841 | 90 | 15,870.52 |
| 1842 | 42 | 4,235.40 | 1842 | 31 | 5,546.72 | 1842 | 22 | 5,607.67 | 1842 | 102 | 16,794.88 |
| 1843 | 17 | 2,817,44 | 1843 | 22 | 4,092.09 | 1843 | 11 | 1,664.18 | 1843 | 55 | 9,385.82 |

| PITTSBURGH | | | CINCINNATI | | | LOUISVILLE | | | WESTERN RIVERS | | |
|---|---|---|---|---|---|---|---|---|---|---|---|
| 1844 | 34 | 6,138.53 | 1844 | 43 | 8,696.77 | 1844 | 35 | 7,165.11 | 1844 | 129 | 25,395.24 |
| 1845 | 46 | 6,504.81 | 1845 | 37 | 7,175.32 | 1845 | 26 | 5,681.01 | 1845 | 119 | 20,104.70 |
| 1846 | 49 | 7,506.89 | 1846 | 29 | 5,266.00 | 1846 | 46 | 8,651.47 | 1846 | 150 | 25,560.32 |
| 1847 | 57 | 9,516.45 | 1847 | 30 | 7,284.42 | 1847 | 30 | 5,340.65 | 1847 | 120 | 22,438.82 |
| 1848 | 42 | 7,237.43 | 1848 | 16 | 5,165.49 | 1848 | 39 | 9,274.60 | 1848 | 120 | 27,271.03 |
| 1849 | 52 | 7,946.01 | 1849 | 38 | 8,475.67 | 1849 | 34 | 8,423.33 | 1849 | 139 | 28,353.24 |
| 1850 | 50 | 8,405.73 | 1850 | 17 | 4,278.91 | 1850 | 34 | 6,460.49 | 1850 | 109 | 20,910.87 |
| 1851 | 51 | 7,601.52 | 1851 | 23 | 6,179.64 | 1851 | 38 | 8,861.49 | 1851 | 132 | 26,711.10 |
| 1852 | 55 | 12,317.81 | 1852 | 45 | 11,117.35 | 1852 | 27 | 7,312.77 | 1852 | 155 | 35,259.24 |
| 1853 | 34 | 7,112.11 | 1853 | 35 | 11,272.58 | 1853 | 30 | 8,592.09 | 1853 | 126 | 33,452.44 |
| 1854 | 61 | 11,333.43 | 1854 | 38 | 9,469.10 | 1854 | 22 | 6,823.71 | 1854 | 142 | 33,805.39 |
| 1855 | 51 | 10,059.35 | 1855 | 19 | 5,670.93 | 1855 | 27 | 9,402.77 | 1855 | 116 | 30,926.03 |
| 1856 | 60 | 12,329.57 | 1856 | 28 | 8,427.51 | 1856 | 18 | 5,642.22 | 1856 | 138 | 32,632.65 |
| 1857 | 70 | 12,929.35 | 1857 | 33 | 9,469.87 | 1857 | 28 | 8,462.46 | 1857 | 163 | 37,080.30 |
| 1858 | 53 | 9,541.13 | 1858 | 20 | 5,646.54 | 1858 | 28 | 8,302.74 | 1858 | 127 | 31,484.40 |
| 1859 | 29 | 4,199.21 | 1859 | 17 | 3,703.46 | 1859 | 19 | 3,702.47 | 1859 | 85 | 13,838.52 |
| 1860 | 69 | 10,811.01 | 1860 | 30 | 5,201.49 | 1860 | 29 | 8,631.78 | 1860 | 162 | 32,432.03 |
| 1861 | 47 | 9,558.25 | 1861 | 31 | 4,327.86 | 1861 | 33 | 9,717.29 | 1861 | 146 | 30,459.07 |
| 1862 | 25 | 3,174.40 | 1862 | 4 | 436.84 | 1862 | 3 | 1,042.32 | 1862 | 49 | 6,653.34 |
| 1863 | 57 | 12,075.72 | 1863 | 35 | 5,708.11 | 1863 | 22 | 5,920.31 | 1863 | 118 | 21,721.76 |
| 1864 | 86 | 17,194.03 | 1864 | 55 | 12,691.90 | 1864 | 15 | 5,530.05 | 1864 | 206 | 44,656.06 |
| 1865 | 66 | 15,845.06 | 1865 | 51 | 15,925.44 | 1865 | 30 | 6,924.76 | 1865 | 187 | 50,081.84 |
| 1866 | 63 | 15,921.70 | 1866 | 40 | 14,389.88 | 1866 | 21 | 7,470.23 | 1866 | 153 | 46,755.49 |
| 1867 | 27 | 9,511.39 | 1867 | 13 | 4,575.79 | 1867 | 20 | 6,834.28 | 1867 | 63 | 18,551.74 |
| 1868 | 20 | 4,728.33 | 1868 | 9 | 1,243.19 | 1868 | 21 | 7,582.63 | 1868 | 93 | 20,742.46 |
| 1869 | 18 | 5,843.88 | 1869 | 6 | 3,460.90 | 1869 | 10 | 3,267.54 | 1869 | 79 | 21,022.75 |
| 1870 | 26 | 9,881.95 | 1870 | 19 | 6,841.35 | 1870 | 28 | 12,138.90 | 1870 | 116 | 35,506.15 |
| 1871 | 37 | 13,844.11 | 1871 | 35 | 14,470.10 | 1871 | 27 | 11,586.02 | 1871 | 155 | 50,083,72 |
| 1872 | 20 | 7,131.95 | 1872 | 23 | 6,118.39 | 1872 | 21 | 7,711.54 | 1872 | 108 | 25,497.63 |
| 1873 | 9 | 1,749.53 | 1873 | 21 | 6,058.29 | 1873 | 17 | 3,302.03 | 1873 | 109 | 19,474.48 |
| 1874 | 23 | 4,810.15 | 1874 | 19 | 3,444.33 | 1874 | 17 | 4,380.01 | 1874 | 125 | 19,672.17 |
| 1875 | 5 | 1,603.61 | 1875 | 16 | 4,007.76 | 1875 | 20 | 2,436.70 | 1875 | 91 | 13,315.80 |
| 1876 | 3 | 829.24 | 1876 | 9 | 2,650.48 | 1876 | 10 | 3,947.92 | 1876 | 109 | 19,025.67 |
| 1877 | 13 | 2,977.62 | 1877 | 11 | 5,108.10 | 1877 | 20 | 6,267.40 | 1877 | 113 | 21,653.54 |
| 1878 | 23 | 8,935.60 | 1878 | 22 | 6,541.89 | 1878 | 25 | 6,471.76 | 1878 | 133 | 28,124.44 |
| 1879 | 16 | 5,967.70 | 1879 | 21 | 7,821.31 | 1879 | 18 | 10,081.26 | 1879 | 124 | 31,539.71 |
| 1880 | 10 | 4,329.74 | 1880 | 18 | 6,484.08 | 1880 | 17 | 5,302.11 | 1880 | 117 | 23,930.92 |

# APPENDIX 2
## TABLE OF STEAMBOAT MEASUREMENTS FROM 1850

*Source:* Walworth, *Order of Reference of the Supreme Court of the United States in the Case of the State of Pennsylvania, Complainant, against the Wheeling & Belmont Bridge Company and Others, Defendants,* pp. 635–39.

| | Buckeye State | Keystone State | Messenger No. 2 | Hibernia No. 2 | Brilliant | Cincinnati | Clipper No. 2 | Paris | Cinderella | Isaac Newton | Geneva |
|---|---|---|---|---|---|---|---|---|---|---|---|
| ngth of deck (feet) | 247 | 250 | 250 | 220 | 227 | 235 | 215 | | 155 | 184 | |
| eadth of beam (feet) | 29 | 38 | 30.5 | 26 | 32 | 29 | 30.5 | 24.5 | 23 | 28.7 | 23.5 |
| pth of hold (feet) | 6.5 | 6 | 6 | 6 | 6 | 6.5 | 5.75 | 6 | 3 | 6 | 4 |
| aft when light (inches) | 41 | 39 | 39 | | 42 | 35 | 40 | | 13 | 33 | 16 |
| ight from water to hurricane deck (feet) | 27 | 26.5 | 26.35 | 25.3 | 26.8 | 27.3 | 26 | 26 | 20.5 | 26 | 21.5 |
| ight from water to top of pilot house (feet) | 46.5 | 45.5 | 46 | 44.5 | 45.8 | 47.3 | 45.5 | 43 | 30 | 43 | 32 |
| ight from water to hinges of chimneys (feet) | 28 | 27.5 | 61 | | 61.3 | 27.8 | 54 | 38 | 45 | 46 | 39.8 |
| ight from water to top of chimneys (feet) | 76 | 77.5 | 71.3 | | 71.3 | 82 | 66.3 | 50.5 | 49 | 59 | 49 |
| ight from water to flues (feet) | 10 | 10 | 9.5 | 9.5 | 9.5 | 10.5 | 9 | 10.5 | | 10 | 8.8 |
| ight of chimney from boiler (feet) | 66 | 67.5 | 61.8 | | 61.8 | 71.5 | 57.3 | 40 | | 49 | 40.3 |
| ameter of chimneys (feet) | 5.6 | 5 | 4.7 | 4.3 | 4.5 | 4.5 | 3.7 | 3.6 | 3.2 | 3.2 | 3.2 |
| e bridge to boilers (inches) | 8 | 6 | 6 | 6 | 5 | 6 | 4 | 6 | 4 | 6 | 4 |
| ilers to back wall (inches) | 9 | 9 | 11 | 10 | 10 | 11 | 9 | 13 | 8.8 | 10 | 9.3 |
| ea for passage of smoke over bridge (square feet) | 26.8 | 20 | 25.5 | 23 | 22.5 | 18.5 | 14 | 13 | 8.8 | 10 | 9.3 |
| ea for passage of smoke behind boilers (square feet) | 15.7 | 12.5 | 19 | 16.2 | 16.7 | 14.7 | 10.9 | 9.2 | 4 | 5.5 | 4.9 |

| | Buckeye State | Keystone State | Messenger No. 2 | Hibernia No. 2 | Brilliant | Cincinnati | Clipper No. 2 | Paris | Cinderella | Isaac Newton | Ge |
|---|---|---|---|---|---|---|---|---|---|---|---|
| 16 Area for passage of smoke through flues (square feet) | 17.6 | 14.1 | 13.9 | 10.7 | 13.9 | 9.8 | 7.3 | 6.4 | 4.2 | 5.5 | 4.9 |
| 17 Area for passage of smoke through britching (square feet) | 36 | 27.5 | 26 | 20.6 | 29.7 | 28 | 17.7 | 15.4 | 12 | 22.7 | 11 |
| 18 Area for passage of smoke through chimneys (square feet) | 49 | 39.2 | 29.5 | 29.5 | 31.8 | 31.8 | 21.1 | 20.1 | 15.7 | 27.2 | 15. |
| 19 Grate: length of bars (feet) | 4 | 4 | 4 | 4 | 4 | 4 | 4 | 4 | 4 | 3.8 | 4 |
| 20 Grate: width across boat (feet) | 21 | 16.7 | 20.8 | 19.5 | 16.7 | 16 | 14.5 | 11 | 8 | 8.3 | 8.5 |
| 21 Grate: area (square feet) | 84 | 67 | 83 | 78 | 66.7 | 64 | 58 | 44 | 32 | 33 | 31. |
| 22 Grate: proportion open | .5 | .5 | .5 | .5 | .5 | .5 | .5 | .38 | .33 | .5 | .25 |
| 23 Grate: height to boilers (inches) | 22 | 22 | 18 | 18 | 22 | 18 | 24 | 18 | 15 | 24 | 18 |
| 24 Boilers: number | 5 | 4 | 5 | 5 | 5 | 4 | 4 | 3 | 2 | 2 | 2 |
| 25 Boilers: length (feet) | 30 | 30 | 28 | 27 | 26.5 | 28 | 26.5 | 24 | 22 | 30 | 22 |
| 26 Boilers: diameter (inches) | 42 | 42 | 42 | 40 | 40 | 42 | 36 | 36 | 38 | 42 | 38 |
| 27 Boilers: fire surface (square feet) | 870 | 705 | 770 | 747 | 734 | 616 | 539 | 369 | 252 | 410 | 239 |
| 28 Boilers: total contents (cubic feet) | 913 | 730 | 956 | 889 | 786 | 803 | 554 | 355 | 252 | 410 | 239 |
| 29 Boilers: thickness of iron (inches) | .25 | .25 | .25 | .25 | .25 | .25 | .25 | .25 | .25 | .25 | .25 |
| 30 Flues: number | 10 | 8 | 10 | 10 | 10 | 8 | 8 | 6 | 4 | 4 | 4 |
| 31 Flues: diameter of each (inches) | 18 | 18 | 16 | 14 | 16 | 15 | 13 | 14 | 14 | 16 | 15 |
| 32 Cylinders: number | 2 | 2 | 2 | 2 | 2 | 2 | 4 | 2 | 2 | 2 | 2 |
| 33 Cylinders: diameter inside (inches) | 29 | 25.5 | 28 | 26 | 26 | 24 | 32 | 18 | 24 | 22 | 12 |
| 34 Cylinders: length of stroke (feet) | 8 | 8 | 7.5 | 8 | 8 | 7 | 7 | 6 | 4 | 7 | 4.5 |
| 35 Water wheels: diameter (feet) | 30 | 30 | 26 | 26 | 30 | 32.5 | 25 | 25 | 14 | 25 | 15 |
| 36 Water wheels: length of bucket (feet) | 11.5 | 12 | 12 | 11.7 | 12 | 11 | 11 | 9.25 | 16 | 9.75 | 18 |
| 37 Water wheels: width of bucket (inches) | 30 | | | 30 | 30 | 28 | 28 | 26 | 18 | 26 | 16 |

| | Buckeye State | Keystone State | Messenger No. 2 | Hibernia No. 2 | Brilliant | Cincinnati | Clipper No. 2 | Paris | Cinderella | Isaac Newton | Geneva |
|---|---|---|---|---|---|---|---|---|---|---|---|
| ual pressure of steam (p.s.i.) | 135 | | 140 | 140 | 150 | | 150 | | 135 | 150 | |
| volutions (per minute) | 19 | 18 | | 19 | 21 | 16 | 18 | | 20 | | |
| el: Coal used in 24 hours (bushels) | 880 | | | | 1075 | 820 | | | 265 | | |
| el: Wood used in 24 hours (cords) | | | | | | | | | | 24 | 22 |
| ual speed upstream (m.p.h.) | | | | | | | | | 6 | 8 | 8 |
| ts off steam at | | | 5/8 | | | | | | | | |

| | Mount Vernon | Hindoo | Pilot No. 2 | Empress | Silas Wright | Louis McLean | Pacific | Caledonia | Citizen | Alleghany Bell | She⟨…⟩ |
|---|---|---|---|---|---|---|---|---|---|---|---|
| 1 Length of deck (feet) | 165 | 175 | | | 175 | 175 | 170 | 145 | 180 | 156 | 182 |
| 2 Breadth of beam (feet) | 27 | 24.5 | 21.5 | 21.5 | 31 | 21 | 22 | 24.5 | 25.5 | 22.5 | 24.⟨ |
| 3 Depth of hold (feet) | 5.5 | 6 | 3.5 | 4 | 6 | 4 | 4 | 3.5 | 4.5 | 3.5 | 4.5 |
| 4 Draft when light (inches) | 27 | 32 | 13 | 18 | | 30 | | 14 | | 24 | 22 |
| 5 Height from water to hurricane deck (feet) | 23.5 | 24 | 20.5 | | 26.5 | 21 | 22.5 | 21.8 | 23.8 | 18 | 23 |
| 6 Height from water to top of pilot house (feet) | 39.3 | 39.5 | 30 | | 45 | 31 | 33 | 32 | 39 | 32.3 | 38.⟨ |
| 7 Height from water to hinges of chimneys (feet) | 24 | 23.5 | 22 | | 48 | 21 | 23.5 | 42.5 | 24.8 | 12.3 | 23 |
| 8 Height from water to top of chimneys (feet) | 58.8 | 55.5 | 48 | | 60 | 49 | 51.5 | 48 | 57.8 | 48 | 49.⟨ |
| 9 Height from water to flues (feet) | 9 | 9.5 | 8.5 | | 10 | 8 | 8 | 8.5 | 9.5 | 6.5 | 9 |
| 10 Height of chimney from boiler (feet) | 49.8 | 46 | 39.5 | | 50 | 41 | 43.5 | 39.5 | 48.3 | 41.5 | 40.⟨ |
| 11 Diameter of chimneys (feet) | 3.2 | 3.3 | 2.1 | | 4 | 3 | 3 | | 3.1 | 4.5 | 3.2 |
| 12 Fire bridge to boilers (inches) | 4 | 6 | 6 | 6 | 8 | 6 | 6 | 6 | 6 | 6 | 6 |
| 13 Boilers to back wall (inches) | 8 | 10 | 8 | 9 | 10 | 10 | 10 | 8 | 8 | 13 | 8 |
| 14 Area for passage of smoke over bridge (square feet) | 7.5 | 13.5 | 8 | 7 | 17.8 | 14.8 | 10 | 10 | 10.5 | 14.5 | 11.5 |
| 15 Area for passage of smoke behind boilers (square feet) | 5 | 9.2 | 4.7 | 5.2 | 10 | 10 | 6.7 | 5.3 | 5.3 | 7.7 | 5.7 |
| 16 Area for passage of smoke through flues (square feet) | 4.2 | 5.5 | 3.8 | 3.1 | 6.4 | 6.4 | 4.2 | 4.2 | 4.2 | 7.3 | 4.9 |
| 17 Area for passage of smoke through britching (square feet) | 12 | 13.5 | 7.8 | 9.3 | 16.5 | 8.7 | 10 | 11 | 12.3 | 12 | 12 |
| 18 Area for passage of smoke through chimneys (square feet) | 15.7 | 17.4 | 10.4 | | 75.1 | 14.1 | 14.1 | | 14.9 | 19.2 | 15.7 |
| 19 Grate: length of bars (feet) | 4 | 4 | 4 | 4 | 4 | 4 | 4 | 4 | 4 | 4 | 4 |
| 20 Grate: width across boat (feet) | 7.5 | 11 | 7 | 7 | 12 | 12 | 8 | 8 | 8 | 11.5 | 8.5 |

| | Mount Vernon | Hindoo | Pilot No. 2 | Empress | Silas Wright | Louis McLean | Pacific | Caledonia | Citizen | Alleghany Belle No. 2 | Shenandoah |
|---|---|---|---|---|---|---|---|---|---|---|---|
| ate: area (square feet) | 30 | 44 | 28 | 28 | 48 | 48 | 32 | 32 | 32 | 46 | 34 |
| ate: proportion open | .5 | .5 | .5 | .38 | .33 | .5 | .33 | .33 | .5 | .38 | .5 |
| ate: height to boilers (inches) | 18 | 18 | 12 | 14 | 19 | 16 | 16 | 16 | 20 | 16 | 16 |
| ilers: number | 2 | 3 | 2 | 2 | 3 | 3 | 2 | 2 | 2 | 3 | 2 |
| ilers: length (feet) | 26 | 22 | 25 | 22.5 | 26 | 22 | 22 | 24 | 24 | 24 | 24 |
| ilers: diameter (inches) | 38 | 34 | 34 | 34 | 38 | 38 | 38 | 38 | 36 | 36 | 38 |
| ilers: fire surface (square feet) | 292 | 317 | 260 | 221 | 438 | 379 | 252 | 272 | 246 | 369 | 272 |
| ilers: total contents (cubic feet) | 298 | 294 | 223 | 213 | 448 | 379 | 252 | 275 | 236 | 332 | 260 |
| ilers: thickness of iron (inches) | .25 | .25 | .25 | .25 | .25 | .25 | .25 | .25 | .25 | .25 | .25 |
| es: number | 4 | 6 | 4 | 4 | 6 | 6 | 4 | 4 | 4 | 6 | 4 |
| es: diameter of each (inches) | 14 | 13 | 13 | 12 | 14 | 14 | 14 | 14 | 14 | 15 | 15 |
| inders: number | 2 | 2 | 2 | 2 | 2 | 2 | 2 | 2 | 2 | 2 | 2 |
| linders: diameter inside (inches) | 15 | 16 | 12 | 9 | 18 | 18 | 12 | 14 | 15 | 16 | 15 |
| linders: length of stroke (feet) | 6 | 6 | 4.5 | 4 | 7 | 7.5 | 5 | 4.5 | 5 | 6 | 5 |
| ater wheels: diameter (feet) | 20 | 23 | 15 | 14 | 24 | 20 | 14 | 15 | 21 | 18 | 21 |
| ater wheels: length of bucket (feet) | 8.5 | 8.5 | 15 | 11 | 9 | 9.5 | 16 | 17.5 | 8 | 17.7 | 8.25 |
| ater wheels: width of bucket (inches) | 20 | 26 | 18 | 18 | 27 | 20 | 18 | 18 | 21 | 24 | 27 |
| ual pressure of steam (p.s.i.) | 135 | 130 | | | | | | | | | |
| volutions (per minute) | | | | | | | | | | | |
| el: Coal used in 24 hours (bushels) | | | | | | 317 | | | | | |
| el: Wood used in 24 hours (cords) | 12 | 18 | | | 35 | | | | | | |
| ual speed upstream (m.p.h.) | 7.5 | 8 | | | 8 | 10 | | 7.5 | | 12 | |
| ts off steam at | | | | | | | | | | | |

| | Tuscarora | Ohio | Alleghany Clipper | Vermont | R. Rogers | Hail Columbia | Glaucus | Beaver | Cumberland No. 2 | James Nelson | Sto |
|---|---|---|---|---|---|---|---|---|---|---|---|
| 1 Length of deck (feet) | 180 | 155 | 136 | 165 | 175 | 155 | | 143 | 153 | 150 | |
| 2 Breadth of beam (feet) | 24 | 24 | 21 | 24 | 26.7 | 23.5 | | 21.5 | 25 | 27 | |
| 3 Depth of hold (feet) | 3.75 | 4 | 3.5 | 5 | 5 | 4 | | 4.5 | 4 | 6 | |
| 4 Draft when light (inches) | 12 | 18 | 21 | 23 | 21 | 18 | | 36 | 16 | 33 | |
| 5 Height from water to hurricane deck (feet) | 22.5 | 21.8 | 20 | 22.8 | 23.3 | 21.3 | 22.5 | 23.3 | 22 | 21 | |
| 6 Height from water to top of pilot house (feet) | 33 | 32 | 30 | 38.8 | 39.8 | 35.7 | 33 | 35.7 | 32 | | |
| 7 Height from water to hinges of chimneys (feet) | 47 | 21.3 | 19.5 | 23.3 | 22.3 | 37.3 | 45.5 | | 46 | 43.5 | |
| 8 Height from water to top of chimneys (feet) | 53 | 56.5 | 50.8 | 55.3 | 54.8 | 51.3 | 53.5 | 59.3 | 52 | 53.5 | 58. |
| 9 Height from water to flues (feet) | 8.25 | 8 | 7.5 | 8.5 | 9.5 | 8 | 7.5 | 8 | 9.5 | 9.5 | 10 |
| 10 Height of chimney from boiler (feet) | 43.8 | 48.5 | 43.3 | 46.8 | 45.3 | 43.3 | 46 | 52.3 | 42.5 | 44 | 48. |
| 11 Diameter of chimneys (feet) | 3 | 3.2 | 3.2 | 3.5 | 3.4 | 3 | 3.2 | 3.75 | 3.5 | 4.2 | |
| 12 Fire bridge to boilers (inches) | 5 | 5 | 6 | 6 | 6 | 6 | 6 | 6 | 6 | 6 | |
| 13 Boilers to back wall (inches) | 8 | 8 | 8 | 8 | 8 | 8 | 8 | 8 | 7 | 8 | |
| 14 Area for passage of smoke over bridge (square feet) | 13 | 10.8 | 13.5 | 8 | 13.3 | 10 | 13.3 | 13.5 | 10 | 14.3 | |
| 15 Area for passage of smoke behind boilers (square feet) | 7.3 | 5.7 | 7.3 | 4.7 | 7.3 | 5.3 | 7.3 | 8 | 4.7 | 8 | |
| 16 Area for passage of smoke through flues (square feet) | 4.7 | 4.9 | 5.5 | 3.7 | 5.5 | 4.9 | | 7.4 | 4.9 | 8.4 | |
| 17 Area for passage of smoke through britching (square feet) | 12 | 12 | 12 | 12 | 15 | 10 | 12 | 14.6 | 13.5 | 24 | |
| 18 Area for passage of smoke through chimneys (square feet) | 14.1 | 15.7 | 15.7 | 19.2 | 18.3 | 14.1 | 15.7 | 22.1 | 14.9 | 27.3 | |
| 19 Grate: length of bars (feet) | 4 | 4 | 4 | 4 | 4 | 4 | 4 | 4 | 4 | 4 | |
| 20 Grate: width across boat (feet) | 11 | 8.5 | 11 | 7 | 11 | 8 | 11 | 12 | 8 | 12 | |

| | Tuscarora | Ohio | Alleghany Clipper | Vermont | R. Rogers | Hail Columbia | Glaucus | Beaver | Cumberland No. 2 | James Nelson | Storm |
|---|---|---|---|---|---|---|---|---|---|---|---|
| ate: area (square feet) | 44 | 34 | 44 | 28 | 44 | 32 | 44 | 48 | 32 | 48 | |
| ate: proportion open | .38 | .5 | .5 | .38 | .62 | .5 | .5 | .5 | .5 | .67 | |
| ate: height to boilers (inches) | 15 | 15 | 12 | 15 | 18 | 16 | 16 | 15 | 21 | 16 | |
| ilers: number | 3 | 2 | 3 | 2 | 3 | 2 | 3 | 3 | 2 | 3 | 3 |
| ilers: length (feet) | 20 | 24 | 24 | 22 | 20 | 22 | 20 | 24 | 24 | 24 | 24 |
| ilers: diameter (inches) | 32 | 38 | 34 | 34 | 34 | 38 | 34 | 40 | 38 | 40 | 42 |
| ilers: fire surface (square feet) | 282 | 272 | 344 | | | | | | | | |
| ilers: total contents (cubic feet) | 241 | 260 | 321 | 196 | | | | | | 427 | 491 |
| ilers: thickness of iron (inches) | .25 | .25 | .25 | .25 | .25 | .25 | .25 | .25 | .25 | .25 | .25 |
| es: number | 4 | 4 | 6 | 4 | 6 | 4 | 6 | 6 | 4 | 6 | 6 |
| es: diameter of each (inches) | 12 | 15 | 13 | 13 | 13 | 15 | | 15 | 15 | 16 | 16 |
| inders: number | 2 | 2 | 2 | 1 | 2 | 2 | 2 | 2 | 2 | 2 | 2 |
| inders: diameter inside (inches) | 14.5 | 14 | 16 | 16 | 16 | 12 | 12 | 18 | 14 | 18 | 20 |
| inders: length of stroke (feet) | 4.5 | 5 | 5 | 6 | 5 | 4 | 4.5 | 6 | 4.5 | 7 | 7 |
| ater wheels: diameter (feet) | 15.5 | 16 | 16 | 20 | 22 | 14 | 16 | 20 | 16 | 22 | 24 |
| ater wheels: length of bucket (feet) | 17.5 | 17.5 | 17.7 | 7.5 | 8 | 16.5 | 17.5 | 18 | 17.5 | 20 | 8.75 |
| ater wheels: width of bucket (inches) | 18 | 18 | 22 | 8 | 23 | 16 | 16 | 30 | 18 | 30 | 30 |
| ual pressure of steam (p.s.i.) | 130 | | 125 | 125 | 150 | | | 130 | | | |
| volutions (per minute) | | | 19 | | | | | | | 20 | |
| el: Coal used in 24 hours (bushels) | 240 | | 336 | | | | | | | | |
| el: Wood used in 24 hours (cords) | 7 | 7 | 12 | 7 | | 7 | | | | | |
| ual speed upstream (m.p.h.) | | | | | | | | | | | |
| ts off steam at | | | | | | | | | | | |

| | | Ironton | G. W. Kendall | New Orleans | Europa | Wisconsin | Peytona | North River | St. Anthony | Hoosier State | Pike No. 9 | So |
|---|---|---|---|---|---|---|---|---|---|---|---|---|
| 1 | Length of deck (feet) | 157 | 182 | 182 | 182 | 200 | 266 | 182 | | 220 | 178 | |
| 2 | Breadth of beam (feet) | 26 | 32 | 36 | 36 | 28 | 34 | | 28 | 30 | 26 | 29 |
| 3 | Depth of hold (feet) | 5.67 | 8 | 8 | 6.5 | 6 | 8 | | 4.5 | 6 | 6.25 | 7 |
| 4 | Draft when light (inches) | | 38 | 42 | 39 | 36 | 42 | 32 | 30 | 42 | | 36 |
| 5 | Height from water to hurricane deck (feet) | | 26.5 | 29 | 29 | 24 | 31 | 25.3 | 21 | 26.3 | 26 | 27 |
| 6 | Height from water to top of pilot house (feet) | | | | | | | | | | | |
| 7 | Height from water to hinges of chimneys (feet) | | 47 | 47 | 48.5 | | | 48.3 | 45 | | 49 | 49 |
| 8 | Height from water to top of chimneys (feet) | 54 | 61 | 63 | 64.5 | 60 | 74 | 60.3 | 51 | 66 | 61 | 61 |
| 9 | Height from water to flues (feet) | 8.25 | 10 | 12.5 | 11.5 | 8 | 11 | 9 | 7 | 9.5 | 10.5 | 11.5 |
| 10 | Height of chimney from boiler (feet) | 45.8 | 51 | 51.5 | 53 | 52 | 63 | 51.3 | 44 | 56.5 | 50.5 | 49. |
| 11 | Diameter of chimneys (feet) | | 4.5 | 3.75 | 4.2 | 3.5 | 5.1 | 4 | 3.2 | 4.5 | 3.6 | 3.6 |
| 12 | Fire bridge to boilers (inches) | | 4 | 6 | 4 | 6 | 9 | 6 | | 4 | 4 | |
| 13 | Boilers to back wall (inches) | | 10 | | 12 | 12 | 18 | 12 | 10 | 12 | 10 | |
| 14 | Area for passage of smoke over bridge (square feet) | | 16 | 19.5 | 15.8 | 11.3 | 34.7 | 15.7 | | 16.8 | 12.5 | |
| 15 | Area for passage of smoke behind boilers (square feet) | | 13.5 | | 13.5 | 16.5 | 36.8 | 12.5 1.2 | | 16.5 | 13.5 | |
| 16 | Area for passage of smoke through flues (square feet) | | 11.2 | 11.2 | 8.4 | 14 | 14.7 | 7.3 | 8.4 | 11.2 | 9.8 | 11.2 |
| 17 | Area for passage of smoke through britching (square feet) | | 24 | 21 | 18.7 | 14 | | 18 | 12.5 | 21.5 | 17.5 | |
| 18 | Area for passage of smoke through chimneys (square feet) | | 28.4 | 22.1 | 27.3 | 19.2 | 40.6 | 25.1 | 15.7 | 31.8 | 20.2 | 21. |
| 19 | Grate: length of bars (feet) | 4 | 4 | 4 | 4 | 4 | 4 | 4 | 4 | 4 | | |
| 20 | Grate: width across boat (feet) | | 16.3 | 16.5 | 13.5 | 16.5 | 24.5 | 12.5 | | 16.5 | 14.5 | |

| | Ironton | G. W. Kendall | New Orleans | Europa | Wisconsin | Peytona | North River | St. Anthony | Hoosier State | Pike No. 9 | South America |
|---|---|---|---|---|---|---|---|---|---|---|---|
| Grate: area (square feet) | | 65 | 66 | 54 | 66 | 98 | 50 | | 66 | 58 | |
| Grate: proportion open | | .33 | .4 | .29 | .6 | .3 | .5 | | .4 | .33 | |
| Grate: height to boilers (inches) | | 17 | 18 | 21 | 16 | 22 | 18 | | 16 | 21 | |
| Boilers: number | 3 | 4 | 4 | 3 | 5 | 6 | 3 | 3 | 4 | 4 | 4 |
| Boilers: length (feet) | 26 | 27 | 30 | 30.5 | 28 | 32.5 | 24 | 24 | 30 | 30 | 30 |
| Boilers: diameter (inches) | 42 | 42 | 42 | 42 | 40 | 42 | 40 | 38 | 42 | 42 | 42 |
| Boilers: fire surface (square feet) | | 594 | 705 | 538 | 773 | 1071 | 413 | 408 | 705 | 705 | 705 |
| Boilers: total contents (cubic feet) | 532 | 737 | 818 | 624 | 878 | 1394 | 451 | 365 | 818 | 857 | 868 |
| Boilers: thickness of iron (inches) | .25 | .38 | .25 | .25 | .25 | .25 | .25 | .25 | .25 | .25 | .25 |
| Flues: number | 6 | 8 | 8 | 6 | 10 | 12 | 6 | 6 | 8 | 8 | 8 |
| Flues: diameter of each (inches) | 16 | 16 | 16 | 16 | 15 | 15 | 15 | 16 | 16 | 15 | 16 |
| Cylinders: number | 2 | 2 | 2 | 2 | 2 | 2 | 2 | 1 | 2 | 2 | 2 |
| Cylinders: diameter inside (inches) | 24 | 24.5 | 24 | 22 | 22.5 | 30.5 | 18 | 22 | 24.5 | 24 | 24 |
| Cylinders: length of stroke (feet) | 7 | 7.5 | 8 | | 8 | 10 | 7 | 7 | 8 | 8 | 8 |
| Water wheels: diameter (feet) | 24 | 30 | 28 | 28 | 27 | 33 | 25 | 21 | 28 | 26 | 25 |
| Water wheels: length of bucket (feet) | 9 | 9.5 | 8.5 | 8.5 | 11.8 | 16 | 9.5 | 9.5 | 13 | 9.5 | 10 |
| Water wheels: width of bucket (inches) | 30 | 36 | 30 | 26 | 31 | 30 | 24 | 24 | 30 | 28 | 26 |
| Usual pressure of steam (p.s.i.) | 130 | 140 | 95 | 125 | 135 | 120 | 100 | 150 | | | |
| Revolutions (per minute) | 25 | 18 | 19 | 20 | 22 | 17 | 17 | 26 | | | |
| Fuel: Coal used in 24 hours (bushels) | | | | | 220 | | | | | | |
| Fuel: Wood used in 24 hours (cords) | | 40 | 40 | 45 | 24 | 64 | 24 | | | | 35 |
| Usual speed upstream (m.p.h.) | | 10 | 7 | 10 | 12 | 12 | 10 | 9 | | | 8 |
| Cuts off steam at | | 5/8 | 1/2 | 1/2 | 1/2 | 1/2 | | 9/16 | 5/8 | 1/2 | |

| | | Cincinnatus | Empire State | Gen. Washington | Simon Kenton | Childe Harold | Yorktown | John Adams | C. J. Marshall | Moro Castle | Telegraph No. | Ben |
|---|---|---|---|---|---|---|---|---|---|---|---|---|
| 1 | Length of deck (feet) | 182 | 182 | 182 | 182 | 182 | 182 | 182 | 1800 | 180 | | 262 |
| 2 | Breadth of beam (feet) | 36 | 36 | 38 | 29 | 34 | 36 | 36 | 33 | 33 | | 33 |
| 3 | Depth of hold (feet) | 8 | 7.25 | 8.5 | 8 | 8 | 8 | 8 | 7 | 7 | | 7 |
| 4 | Draft when light (inches) | | 36 | | | 48 | 48 | 48 | 42 | 36 | | 48 |
| 5 | Height from water to hurricane deck (feet) | 29.5 | 30 | 28.3 | 24 | 28.5 | 29 | 29.5 | 27.8 | 26.5 | 26.3 | 29.5 |
| 6 | Height from water to top of pilot house (feet) | | | | | | | | | 44.5 | | |
| 7 | Height from water to hinges of chimneys (feet) | 49.5 | 49.5 | 48.3 | 46 | 48.5 | 49 | 49.5 | 47.8 | 46.5 | 28 | |
| 8 | Height from water to top of chimneys (feet) | 63.5 | 63.5 | 62.3 | 60 | 62.5 | 61 | 63.5 | 57.8 | 58.5 | 79.8 | 80. |
| 9 | Height from water to flues (feet) | 12 | 11.5 | 11.5 | 9 | 11.5 | 13 | 12 | 10 | 11.5 | 9 | 10 |
| 10 | Height of chimney from boiler (feet) | 51.5 | 52 | 50.8 | 51 | 51 | 48 | 51.5 | 47.8 | 47 | 70.8 | 70.5 |
| 11 | Diameter of chimneys (feet) | 4.4 | 3.67 | 4.4 | 3.75 | 3.8 | 3.5 | 3.8 | 4.25 | 3.67 | | 4.5 |
| 12 | Fire bridge to boilers (inches) | 6 | 4 | 6 | 8 | 6 | 4 | 5 | 6 | 6 | 6 | 8 |
| 13 | Boilers to back wall (inches) | | 12 | 12 | 12 | 9 | 12 | 11 | 8 | 9 | | |
| 14 | Area for passage of smoke over bridge (square feet) | 13.5 | 14.3 | 18 | 17.6 | 17 | 16.8 | 14 | 19 | 15 | 19.7 | 25 |
| 15 | Area for passage of smoke behind boilers (square feet) | | 13 | 16 | 15 | 11.3 | 16.5 | 13.8 | 10.7 | 9.5 | | |
| 16 | Area for passage of smoke through flues (square feet) | 8.4 | 8.4 | 9.8 | 9.8 | 8.5 | 11.2 | 8.5 | 11.2 | 8.4 | 14 | 12.8 |
| 17 | Area for passage of smoke through britching (square feet) | 20 | 20 | 20 | 15 | 20 | 20 | 18.7 | 27.0 | 14 | 21.5 | 27 |
| 18 | Area for passage of smoke through chimneys (square feet) | 21.1 | 30.6 | 22.1 | 23.1 | 23.1 | 19.2 | 23.1 | 28.4 | 21.1 | | 31.8 |
| 19 | Grate: length of bars (feet) | 4 | 4 | 4 | 4 | 4 | 4 | 4 | 4 | 4 | 4 | 4 |
| 20 | Grate: width across boat (feet) | 12 | 13 | 16 | 15 | 15 | 16.5 | 15 | 16 | 12.5 | 19 | 22 |

| | Cincinnatus | Empire State | Gen. Washington | Simon Kenton | Childe Harold | Yorktown | John Adams | C. J. Marshall | Moro Castle | Telegraph No. 2 | Ben Franklin |
|---|---|---|---|---|---|---|---|---|---|---|---|
| Grate: area (square feet) | 48 | 52 | 64 | 60 | 60 | 66 | 60 | 64 | 50 | 76 | 88 |
| Grate: proportion open | .33 | .25 | .5 | .33 | .38 | .5 | .33 | .5 | .5 | .5 | .5 |
| Grate: height to boilers (inches) | 22 | 20 | 19 | 16 | 21 | 22 | 21 | 20 | 20 | 22 | 22 |
| Boilers: number | 3 | 3 | 4 | 4 | 4 | 4 | 4 | 4 | 3 | 5 | 6 |
| Boilers: length (feet) | 32 | 28 | 29 | 26 | 32 | 30 | 30 | 28 | 30 | 30 | 32 |
| Boilers: diameter (inches) | 42 | 42 | 42 | 42 | 38 | 42 | 42 | 40 | 42 | 42 | 42 |
| Boilers: fire surface (square feet) | 575 | 616 | 681 | 611 | 684 | 705 | 705 | 619 | 529 | 870 | 1150 |
| Boilers: total contents (cubic feet) | 655 | 573 | 831 | 745 | 734 | 817 | 896 | 664 | 614 | 1025 | 1436 |
| Boilers: thickness of iron (inches) | .25 | .25 | .25 | .25 | .25 | .25 | .25 | .25 | .25 | .25 | .25 |
| Flues: number | 6 | 6 | 8 | 8 | 8 | 8 | 8 | 8 | 6 | 10 | 12 |
| Flues: diameter of each (inches) | 16 | 16 | 15 | 15 | 14 | 16 | 14 | 16 | 16 | 16 | 14 |
| Cylinders: number | 2 | 2 | 2 | 2 | 2 | 2 | 2 | 2 | 2 | 2 | 2 |
| Cylinders: diameter inside (inches) | 22 | 20 | 23 | 23 | 24 | 24 | 24 | 24 | 18.5 | | 30 |
| Cylinders: length of stroke (feet) | 8 | 6.5 | 8 | 7.5 | 8 | 9 | 8 | 7 | 9 | 9 | 8 |
| Water wheels: diameter (feet) | 28 | 26 | 26 | 25 | 29 | 29.5 | 27 | 29 | 27 | 30 | 27 |
| Water wheels: length of bucket (feet) | 8.5 | 8 | 8.5 | 10 | 14 | 9 | 9 | 9.5 | 9.5 | 12.5 | 9 |
| Water wheels: width of bucket (inches) | 30 | 30 | 27 | 30 | 36 | 28 | 30 | 30 | 30 | 35 | 36 |
| Usual pressure of steam (p.s.i.) | 135 | 135 | 135 | 120 | 120 | 125 | 135 | 135 | 130 | | 90 |
| Revolutions (per minute) | 18 | 20 | | 20 | 17 | 18 | 18 | 20 | | 17 | 20 |
| Fuel: Coal used in 24 hours (bushels) | | | | 400 | | | | | | | |
| Fuel: Wood used in 24 hours (cords) | 35 | 31 | 25 | 24 | 36 | 28 | 30 | 30 | 30 | | 36 |
| Usual speed upstream (m.p.h.) | 8 | 8 | 8 | 12 | 9 | 10 | 8 | | 9 | | 12 |
| Cuts off steam at | | 5/8 | 5/8 | 5/8 | 1/2 | 5/8 | 5/8 | 1/2 | 5/8 | 5/8 | 5/8 |

# GLOSSARY

abaft
:   a directional term meaning "toward the stern"

after
:   behind

alluvial
:   relating to or composed of clay, silt, sand, gravel, or similar detrital material deposited by running water

amidships
:   located in the center of a vessel

arm
:   the spoke of a paddle wheel

bar
:   a riverbed obstruction composed of sand or gravel

beam
:   width of the hull

berths
:   cabins containing one or more beds, or the beds themselves

bilge
:   bottom of the hull of a boat

bilge pump
:   device for pumping water out a of boat's hold

bilge streaks
:   longitudinally oriented timbers that run on the tops of the frames (or ribs) of a boat

boiler
:   metal tank filled with water that is heated to produce steam that then powers the engine

boiler deck
:   the second deck; the one above the boilers

bow
:   the forward part of a boat

bowsprit
:   forward-angling spar in the bow of a vessel to which the head gear (sails and rigging) are attached

braces
:   timber posts used in connection with the hog-chain system to hold the hull in shape

breeching
  sheet metal connecting the boilers and the chimneys
bucket
  the paddle of a paddle wheel
bulkhead
  a partition or wall
cabin
  an interior room containing sleeping berths
canted
  angled
camber
  the athwartships curve of a deck
capstan
  a rotating cylinder oriented vertically and used for lifting anchors or
  hauling cables
chimney
  sheet-metal tube used to carry smoke away from the vessel and create a
  draft in the furnace
chine
  an angular meeting between the bottom and sides of the hull
cocked hat
  a triangular wooden block used to brace paddle-wheel arms; a triangular
  timber used to brace the floors and futtocks where the bottom of the hull
  meets the sides
collar
  lead washer used to make boiler joints steam tight
compass timber
  a curved timber in boat construction derived from the similarly curved
  portions of a tree
condensing engine
  a type of steam engine, normally of low pressure, that condenses the
  steam in the cylinder
cordelling
  method used to move a keelboat in which the crew towed the vessel from
  the riverbank
cotton packet
  a side-wheel or stern-wheel steamboat modified to carry cotton, with an
  extra-wide main deck and very narrow boiler deck and cabin
counter stern
  type of stern with an arch forming an overhang abaft the sternpost
crank
  the bent part of a shaft or axle through which reciprocating motion is
  transformed into rotary motion, or vice versa

cross chains
   a system of wrought-iron rods used to hold up the guards
cutoff valve
   a valve designed to cut off live steam prior to the piston reaching the end
   of its stroke
cylinder
   the heart of a steam engine; steam expands in the cylinder, pushing the
   piston and moving the paddle wheel
cylinder timbers
   a long structural member that supported the engine cylinder and paddle-
   wheel shaft
deadrise
   the upward angle of a floor in the hull
death hook
   a hook on the end of a safety-valve lever from which the engineer could
   hang weights to increase steam pressure
deck beam
   transversely oriented framing on which decking is affixed
depth of hull
   the distance from the bottom of the keel to the underside of the deck
   beam
doctor
   auxiliary engine used either to pump water to the boilers or to work the
   bilge pumps or fire hoses
draft
   the amount of hull extending into the water as measured vertically
figurehead
   the figure on a ship's bow
firebox
   the compartment where wood or coal was burned in order to heat
   the boilers
flange
   the metal ring surrounding the end of a flue by which it was connected to
   the boiler head; the hub on a paddle wheel where the arms are attached
floors
   the bottommost portion of the frames or ribs of a ship
flue
   an iron tube running through the boiler for the purposes of conveying
   hot gases and heating the water more rapidly
fluvial
   produced by the action of a river or stream
furnace
   the space under the boilers where the fire is built

futtocks
> the separate pieces of timber that form the frames of a ship

garboard
> planks directly adjacent to the keel

gauge cocks
> valves located on the boiler head used for monitoring the water level inside the boiler, also known as try cocks

grummets
> lead washers used to make boiler joints steamtight

guards
> portion of the deck that overhangs the side of the vessel

high-pressure engine
> a steam engine powered by the expansive force of high-pressure steam injected into the engine's cylinder

hogging
> the tendency for a hull to hump up in the center and droop at the ends

hog chain
> an iron rod passing over braces, used to prevent the hull from hogging or sagging

hold
> the interior space of a the hull, used for cargo

hold streak
> longitudinally oriented timbers that run on the tops of the frames (or ribs) of a boat

hull
> the outer shell of a vessel exclusive of masts, yards, sails, and rigging

hurricane deck
> the third deck, located above the boiler deck

iron circle
> the iron reinforcing ring that extends around the diameter of a paddle wheel, just inside the bucket planks, to strengthen the structure

keel
> longitudinal timber that extends the length of the bottom of the vessel, forming the backbone of the vessel

keel plank
> a keel that is the same size or only slightly larger than the garboard planks to either side

keelson
> an interior longitudinal timber that runs along the centerline of the vessel and rests on top of the frames or ribs

key
> a blunt wedge used for adjustment of a wooden or metal structure

knee
a timber hewn or grown into a right angle to provide strengthening and
support at the points of intersection of a boat's timbers
knuckle chains
an iron rod used to hold up the sides of the hull
leeway
the tendency of sailing vessels to be pushed downwind rather than the
desired direction
lines
the shape of a hull
low-pressure engine
an engine type powered by a low pressure of steam, the driving force
coming from the application a partial vacuum formed in the cylinder
main deck
the lowest external deck, which covers the hull
manhole
a hole in the boiler head through which the boiler can be cleaned or
inspected
mast
any upright spar
model bow
a sharp bow
mortice
recess carved into a timber for the purpose of fitting another timber
moulded
the height of a timber in the hull
mud drum
a cylindrical container below the boilers used to collect sediment
outboard
in a lateral direction from the hull
oxbow lake
a river bend that has been cut off to form a lake
packet boat
a vessel carrying passengers and freight, equipped for overnight trips
pilothouse
uppermost compartment of the steamboat, from which the pilot steers
the vessel
pitman
the connecting rod between the engine crosshead and the paddle-
wheel crank
plans
drawing showing the construction or shape of a vessel

planter
> a snag that is fixed to the riverbed

pocket
> recess within a paddle-wheel flange is used to secure the paddle-wheel arm

poling
> method used to move a keelboat in which the crewmen set their poles against the river bottom and walk along the edge of the deck from bow to stern

quarter deck
> that part of the upper deck of a boat abaft the mainmast, or approximately where the mainmast would be in the case of vessels without one

rockered keel
> a keel that bends upward at the bow and stern

room and space
> the distance between floors

rudder
> a hinged plate at the stern of a vessel used to control its direction

safety valve
> a relief valve that opened when the boiler pressure exceeded a predetermined amount

saloon
> the large hallway that ran the length of the boiler deck

sawyer
> a snag whose upper end moves up and down in the water column

scantlings
> timbers used in boat construction

schooner
> a type of oceangoing vessel rigged principally with fore and aft sails

scow bow
> a square, raking bow

scuttle
> to intentionally sink a vessel

sheer
> the graceful swooping curve of the upper hull when seen from the side

sheer strake
> uppermost stake in the hull

shoal
> shallow-water area in a river or other body of water

sided
> the width of a timber in the hull

side-wheeler
> type of steamboat in which a paddle wheel was located on each side of the hull

snag
  a tree in the riverbed forming an obstruction to navigation
snag chamber
  a sealed chamber within the bow used to prevent the entire hull from
  flooding in the event of a rupture by a snag
spoonbill bow
  type of steamboat bow with full lines
stanchion
  vertical framing post supporting a deck
steam drum
  a cross pipe above the boilers used for collecting and distributing steam
stem
  the foremost timber in the hull
sternpost
  the aftermost timber in the hull
stern-wheeler
  type of steamboat in which a single paddle wheel is located at the stern
superstructure
  the decks and structure above the main deck
*terminus post quem*
  the date after which an archaeological feature must have been deposited
Texas
  a series of cabins located above the hurricane deck
trans-Appalachian West
  lands west of the Appalachian Mountains
transom
  the athwartships timbers bolted to the sternpost to give a boat a flat stern
turn of the bilge
  the portion of the hull where the sides meet the bottom
turnbuckle
  a slotted casting with threaded holes used to tighten hog, cross, or
  knuckle chains
warping
  method used to move a keelboat in which a rope was attached to a
  fixed point and the vessel was pulled along that rope using a capstan
  or windlass
windlass
  a horizontally oriented cylinder on a vessel's deck used to pull in lines
  or cable

# NOTES

## Introduction

1. Charles Dickens, *American Notes and Pictures from Italy*, pp. 156–57.
2. George Armroyd, *A Connected View of the Whole Internal Navigation of the United States*, p. 364; G. S. Callender, "The Early Transportation and Banking Enterprises of the States in Relation to the Growth of Corporations," *Quarterly Journal of Economics* 17 (Nov., 1902): 128–29; James Hall, *The West: Its Commerce and Navigation*, p. 41; James Hall, *Statistics of the West at the Close of the Year 1836*, pp. 236–38; Louis. C. Hunter, *Steamboats on the Western Rivers: An Economic and Technological History*, p. 3; J. H. Lanman, "American Steam Navigation," *Hunt's Merchants' Magazine* 4 (1841): 124; George Neff, *Proceedings of a Meeting of the Citizens of Cincinnati Held at the Council Chamber, January 22, 1846, Expressing the Sense of the Citizens on the Subject of Improving the Navigation around the Falls of the Ohio River*, p. 12; Oscar O. Winther, *The Transportation Frontier: Trans-Mississippi West, 1865–1890*, pp. 74–75.
3. George R. Taylor, *The Transportation Revolution: 1815–1860*, p. 63.

## Chapter 1

1. Thomas Allen, A. B. Chambers, N. J. Eaton, George K. McGunnegle, Wilson Primm, Samuel Treat, and James E. Yeatman, *The Commerce and Navigation of the Valley of the Mississippi; and also that Appertaining to the City of St. Louis: Considered, with Reference to the Improvement, by the General Government, of the Mississippi River and Its Principal Tributaries*, p. 4.
2. Drew R. McCoy, *The Elusive Republic: Political Economy in Jeffersonian America*, p. 62.
3. R. E. Ellis, "The Political Economy of Thomas Jefferson," in *Thomas Jefferson: The Man, His World, His Influence*, ed., Weymouth, p. 84.
4. Samuel White, "New, Immense, Unbounded World," *Annals of Congress*, 8th Cong., 1st sess. (1804): 33–34; Donald. W. Meinig, *The Shaping of America: A Geographical Perspective on 500 Years of History, Volume 2, Continental America, 1800–1867*, p. 13.
5. William F. Gephart asserts, "Other things being equal, the rapidity with which a new country becomes settled is directly proportional to its supply of navigable waterways." *Transportation and Industrial Development in the Middle West*, p. 57.
6. Henry C. Adams, *Report on the Transportation Business in the United States at the Eleventh Census: 1890. Part II—Transportation by Water*, p. 415.
7. Isaac Lippincott, *A History of Manufactures in the Ohio Valley to the Year 1860*, p. 56; Hall, *Statistics of the West*, p. 225; David Stevenson, *Sketch of the*

*Civil Engineering of North America*, p. 217. See also Carl D. Arfwedson, *The United States and Canada in 1832, 1833, and 1834*, pp. 47–48.

8. John L. Ringwalt, *Development of Transportation Systems in the United States*, p. 21; Isaac Lippincott, "Pioneer Industry in the West," *The Journal of Political Economy* 18 (Apr., 1910): 270.

9. Erick F. Haites, *Ohio and Mississippi River Transportation, 1810–1860*, p. 25; Armroyd, *Connected View*, p. 364; Allen et al., *Commerce and Navigation of the Valley of the Mississippi*, p. 6.

10. The term "flatboat" is one of several names for this type of vessel. Flatboats were often referred to based on their point of origin, such as Kentucky boats, New Orleans boats, and Arkansas boats. Other vernacular terms, including barges, arks, boxes, tobacco boats, and broad-horns, were also used. See H. E. Hoagland, "Early Transportation on the Mississippi," *The Journal of Political Economy* 19 (Feb., 1911).

11. Leland D. Baldwin, *The Keelboat Age on Western Waters*, p. 48; Haites, *Ohio and Mississippi River Transportation*, p. 28; James Mak and Gary M. Walton, "The Persistence of Old Technologies: The Case of Flatboats," *Journal of Economic History* 33 (June, 1973): 449.

12. Grant Foreman, "River Navigation in the Early Southwest," *The Mississippi Valley Historical Review* 15 (June, 1928): 34; Baldwin, *Keelboat Age*, p. 45; James Hall, *Sketches of History, Life, and Manners, in the West*, Volume II, p. 72.

13. Baldwin, *Keelboat Age*, p. 65.

14. Erick F. Haites, James Mak, and Gary M. Walton, *Western River Transportation: The Era of Early Internal Development, 1810–1860*, p. 20.

15. See Charles G. Sellers, *The Market Revolution: Jacksonian America, 1815–1846;* Douglas C. North, *The Economic Growth of the United States, 1790–1860;* and O. Handlin and M. F. Handlin, *Commonwealth: A Study of the Role of Government in the American Economy: Massachusetts, 1774–1861.*

16. Joyce O. Appleby, *Capitalism and a New Social Order: The Republican Vision of the 1790s*, p. 34.

17. Callender, "Early Transportation and Banking Enterprises," p. 121.

18. Ibid., p. 123; Lippincott, *Manufactures in the Ohio Valley*, p. 58.

19. Callender, "Early Transportation and Banking Enterprises," pp. 116–17; Taylor, *Transportation Revolution*, p. 5; Gottfried Duden, *Report on a Journey to the Western States of North America (during the Years 1824, '25, '26, and 1827)*, p. 192; Thomas M. Monroe, *Remarks of Thomas M. Monroe, of Dubuque, Iowa, before the National Board of Trade*, p. 16.

20. Emerson W. Gould, *Fifty Years on the Mississippi; or, Gould's History of River Navigation*, pp. 101–10.

21. Hall, *Statistics of the West*, p. 239; Armroyd, *Connected View*, p. 364.

22. R. Hyde Walworth, *Order of Reference of the Supreme Court of the United States in the Case of the State of Pennsylvania, Complainant, against the Wheeling &*

*Belmont Bridge Company and Others, Defendants,* pp. 630, 656 [cited hereafter as *The Wheeling Bridge Case*].

23. T. C. Prudy, *Report on Steam Navigation in the United States,* p. 13–14; Eric Haites and James Mak, "The Decline of Steamboating on the Antebellum Western Rivers: Some New Evidence and an Alternative Hypothesis," *Explorations in Economic History* 11 (Fall, 1973): 29. For Prudy's table on steamboat construction on the western rivers, see appendix 1.

24. Erick F. Haites and James Mak, "Social Savings Due to Western River Steamboats," *Research in Economic History* 3 (1978): 263–304; James Mak and Gary M. Walton, "Steamboats and the Great Productivity Surge in River Transportation," *Journal of Economic History* 3 (Sept., 1972): 623; Hunter, *Steamboats on the Western Rivers,* pp. 492–94; Haites, Mak, and Walton, *Western River Transportation,* p. 120.

25. Callender, "Early Transportation and Banking Enterprises," pp. 124, 129–30.

26. See North, *Economic Growth of the United States,* pp. 75–100. Cotton constituted 39 percent of the value of U.S. exports between 1816 and 1820, 63 percent from 1836 to 1840, and approximately 50 percent thereafter, up to the Civil War.

27. Callender, "Early Transportation and Banking Enterprises," p. 126.

28. North, *Economic Growth of the United States,* p. 102.

29. Meinig, *Shaping of America,* p. 222; Allen et al., *Commerce and Navigation of the Valley of the Mississippi,* p. 6. The population of the Mississippi valley in 1800 did not exceed 200,000; in 1800 it increased to approximately 560,000; in 1810 to 1,370,000; in 1820 to 2,580,000; in 1830 to 4,190,000; in 1840 to 6,370,000; and in 1850 to 10,520,000. Ibid., p. 4.

30. Callender, "Early Transportation and Banking Enterprises," p. 130; Hunter, *Steamboats on the Western Rivers,* p. 30.

31. Ringwalt, *Development of Transportation Systems,* p. 114.

32. Stevenson, *Civil Engineering of North America,* p. 76.

33. Hunter, *Steamboats on the Western Rivers,* p. 31.

34. Hall, *Statistics of the West,* pp. 247–48.

35. Hunter, *Steamboats on the Western Rivers,* p. 107; John Law, C. I. Battell, Hamilton Smith, Elisha Embree, Isaac Hutchinson, John Ingle, and M. J. Bray, "Memorial from a Meeting of Citizens of the West, Held at Evansville, Indiana, on the Subject of Western Interests," *House Documents* 31st Cong., 2d sess., 3 (1850): 5.

36. Francis Anthony Chevalier de Gerstner, "Letters from the United States of North America on Internal Improvements, Steam Navigation, Banking, &c.," *Journal of the Franklin Institute* 1 (Feb., 1841): 80; Jack Custer, "Building a Steamboat," *Egregious Steamboat Journal* 31 (1997): 26; Charles Ward, "Shallow-Draught River Steamers," *Transactions of the Society of Naval Architects and Ma-*

*rine Engineers* 17 (1909): 79; Isaac Harris, *Harris' Pittsburgh Business Directory for the Year 1837,* p. 279.

37. Gould, *Fifty Years,* p. 162; Lippincott, *Manufactures in the Ohio Valley,* p. 97; Jeremy Atack, Fred Bateman, and Thomas Weiss, "The Regional Diffusion and Adoption of the Steam Engine in American Manufacturing," *Journal of Economic History* 40 (June, 1980): 287.

38. Henry Hall, *Report on the Ship-Building Industry of the United States,* p. 174, 243.

39. Ibid., p. 188; Anonymous, "Steamboats on the Western Waters," *Journal of the Franklin Institute* 14 (Nov., 1834): 354.

40. Walworth, *The Wheeling Bridge Case,* p. 220 (information compiled by Mr. Charles Ellet Jr.); Charles Mackay, *Life and Liberty in America: or, Sketches of a Tour in the United States and Canada, in 1857-8,* p. 243.

41. Walworth, *The Wheeling Bridge Case,* p. 446.

42. Ward, "Shallow-Draught River Steamers," p. 79. This statistic varies from source to source, with the actual navigable mileage varying from season to season and year to year.

43. Stephen H. Long, "Extent of Steam Navigation on the Western Waters, Including the Rivers, Bayous, &c., Connected with the Mississippi by Channels Navigable for Steamers," *Journal of the Franklin Institute* 15 (May, 1848): 354-55.

44. Samuel H. Gilman, "Steamboats on the Western Waters," *Journal of the Franklin Institute* 24 (Sept., 1852): 207-208.

45. Harriet Martineau, *Retrospect of Western Travel,* pp. 181-82.

46. Hall, *The West,* p. 59; Stevenson, *Civil Engineering of North America,* p. 108; House of Representatives, *Report of the Board of Engineers, on the Ohio and Mississippi Rivers,* p. 21. See also Francesco Arese, *A Trip to the Prairies and the Interior of North America (1837-1838),* pp. 49-50; and Tilly Buttrick, *Voyages, Travels & Discoveries of Tilly Buttrick, Jr.,* pp. 59-60.

47. Hunter, *Steamboats on the Western Rivers,* p. 234.

48. Walworth, *The Wheeling Bridge Case,* p. 230 (testimony of Edwin F. Johnson); William G. Lyford, *The Western Address Directory,* p. 84; House, *Report of the Board of Engineers,* p. 8; Hall, *The West,* p. 53.

49. Hunter, *Steamboats on the Western Rivers,* p. 229.

50. Ibid., p. 182; House, *Report of the Board of Engineers,* p. 9; Walworth, *The Wheeling Bridge Case,* p. xxxi.

51. Annalies Corbin, *The Material Culture of Steamboat Passengers: Archaeological Evidence from the Missouri River,* p. 5; Annalies Corbin, "Shifting Sand and Muddy Water: Historic Cartography and River Migration as Factors in Locating Steamboat Wrecks on the Far Upper Missouri River," *Historical Archaeology* 32, no. 4 (1998): 86.

52. House, *Report of the Board of Engineers,* p. 18.

## Chapter 2

1. Steamboats that have been located but not documented as of fall 2002 are not included in this study.

2. See William B. Lees and J. Barto Arnold III, "Preliminary Assessment of a Wreck in the Red River, Choctaw County, Oklahoma, USA," *The International Journal of Nautical Archaeology* 29, no. 1 (2000): 120–25. Kevin Crisman also supplied data on the Red River Wreck from a documentation project on the vessel undertaken by the Oklahoma Historical Society and the Institute of Nautical Archaeology in the fall of 2002.

3. See Jack Irion, *Archaeological Testing of the Confederate Obstructions, 1Mb28, Mobile Harbor, Alabama.* Data on *Cremona* is included in this study with some reservations. The vessel's identification is based largely on the strength of a Civil War–era map detailing the steamboat's location relative to other vessels sunk by Confederate forces as obstructions. The field measurements are inconsistent with the recorded dimensions of *Cremona,* and the construction of the vessel, which is indistinguishable from that expected of a timber-sided scow barge, is unlike any other steamboat included in this study. But based on the investigator's strong assertion that the most logical identification of the remains is *Cremona,* I have elected to include it in the study.

4. See Charles E. Pearson and Thomas C. C. Birchett, *The History and Archaeology of Two Civil War Steamboats: The Ironclad Gunboat USS* Eastport *and the Steamer* Ed. F. Dix.

5. See Corbin, *Material Culture of Steamboat Passengers;* and Greg Hawley, *Treasure in a Cornfield: The Discovery and Excavation of the Steamboat* Arabia.

6. Adam I. Kane, Jean B. Pelletier, Martha Williams, David S. Robinson, and Roger Saucier, *A Cultural Resources Survey of Items 3B-2 and 4 of the Upper Yazoo River Projects, Leflore County, Mississippi;* Steven R. James, Michael C. Krivor, Alan Whitehead, Kristen Zoelmer, and Michael C. Tuttle, *National Register of Historic Places Eligibility Evaluations of Sites 22Lf966, 22Lf967, and 22Lf969, Limited Survey, and National Register of Historic Places Eligibility Evaluations of All Bridges, Structures, and Revisited Targets Located within Items 3 and 4 of the Upper Yazoo Projects, Yazoo River, Leflore County, Mississippi.*

7. See R. Christopher Goodwin, John L. Seidel, David S. Robinson, Adam I. Kane, and Martha R. Williams, *Phase II and III Archeological Investigations of the Shipwreck* Kentucky *(Site 16BO358) at Eagle Bend, Pool 5, Red River Waterway, Bossier Parish, Louisiana.*

8. See Kane et al., *Survey of Items 3B-2 and 4;* and James et al., *Evaluations of Sites 22Lf966, 22Lf967, and 22Lf969.*

9. See Charles E. Pearson and Allen R. Saltus, *Underwater Archaeology on the Ouachita River, Arkansas: The Search for the* Chieftain, Haydee, *and* Homer.

10. See C. B. Kloppe, Andrew W. Hall, and Joe J. Simmons, *The* A. S. Ruthven.

11. See Robert L. Gearhart and Steven D. Hoyt, *Channel to Liberty: Underwater Archaeological Investigations, Liberty County, Texas;* and Stephen R. James and Charles E. Pearson, *Submerged Cultural Resources Investigations of the Steamboat J. D. Hinde (41LB85), Channel to Liberty, Liberty County, Texas.*

12. See Pearson and Birchett, *History and Archaeology of Two Civil War Steamboats.*

13. See Jerome E. Petsche, *The Steamboat* Bertrand: *History, Excavation, and Architecture.*

14. See R. M Adams, *The Black Cloud Survey.*

15. See David L. Hedrick, *The Investigation of the Caney Creek Shipwreck Archaeological Site 41MG32.*

16. See Charles E. Pearson, "Underwater Archaeology along the Lower Pearl River, Mississippi and Louisiana," *Mississippi Archaeology* 36 (Winter, 2001).

17. See Allen R. Saltus, George J. Castille, and Charles E. Pearson, *Natchez under the Hill: Historical and Archaeological Investigation of Watercraft along the Mississippi River, Adams County, Mississippi.*

18. Leslie C. Stewart-Abernathy, *Ghost Boats on the Mississippi: Discovering Our Working Past.*

19. See Walworth, *The Wheeling Bridge Case.*

20. Two books by Alan Bates, much of whose knowledge comes from actually working on these boats, proved especially useful in understanding the structure and machinery of the western river steamboat. See Bates, *The Western Rivers Engineroom Cyclopoedium;* and *The Western Rivers Steamboat Cyclopoedium.* Other useful secondary sources are Jack Custer, *Egregious Steamboat Journal;* Emerson W. Gould, *Fifty Years on the Mississippi; or Gould's History of River Navigation;* Seymour Dunbar, *A History of Travel in America;* and John H. Morrison, *History of American Steam Navigation.*

## Chapter 3

1. J. Latrobe, *The First Steamboat Voyage on the Western Waters,* pp. 11–12; Morrison, *History of American Steam Navigation,* pp. 190, 192; Latrobe, *First Steamboat Voyage,* p. 12; Albert S. Bolles, *Industrial History of the United States,* p. 558. See also Leland D. Baldwin, "Shipbuilding on the Western Waters, 1793–1817," *The Mississippi Valley Historical Review* 20 (June, 1933): 29–44.

2. Hunter, *Steamboats on the Western Rivers,* p. 67. See also Jean B. Marestier, *Memoir on Steamboats of the United States of America,* p. 7.

3. Hunter, *Steamboats on the Western Rivers,* p. 9.

4. Hall, *Statistics of the West,* p. 230; Alfred R. Maass, "Daniel French and the Western Steamboat Engine," *American Neptune* 56 (Winter, 1996): 35–36; Gould, *Fifty Years,* p. 167; Maass, "Daniel French and the Western Steamboat Engine," p. 32.

5. Marestier, *Memoir on Steamboats,* p. 9; Edouard de Montulé, *Travels in America, 1816–1817,* p. 101; Morrison, *History of American Steam Navigation,*

p. 218. This information is from a letter written by *Vesuvius*'s agent, Jasper Lynch, in 1836. *Vesuvius* caught fire in New Orleans in 1816. It is unclear if the vessel was rebuilt or if an entirely new boat bearing the same name was constructed.

6. Stephen Vail, "Accidents on Board of Steam Boats," in U.S. House of Representatives, *List of Accidents from Bursting of Boilers, on Board of Steam Boats, upon the Mississippi, and Its Tributaries*, p. 14; Montulé, *Travels in America*, pp. 102–103. In Vail's letter to the secretary of the Treasury, *Vesuvius* was listed as having a low-pressure engine. In a letter by an "old timer" regarding steamboat engines from 1812 to 1826, *Vesuvius* is mentioned as having a low-pressure condensing engine on the Boulton and Watt plan. Gould, *Fifty Years*, p. 167.

7. Montulé, *Travels in America*, p. 104; Gould, *Fifty Years*, p. 167; Walworth, *The Wheeling Bridge Case*, p. 541.

8. Maass, "Daniel French and the Western Steamboat Engine," p. 36. Research sources about the dimensions of *Enterprise* are contradictory. Marestier states, "this boat, or one of the same name, is 24.38 meters [80 feet] long, 9.14 meters [30 feet] beam, 3.66 meters [12 feet] depth of hull." *Memoir on Steamboats*, p. 59. His dimensions, though, are too large for a vessel of forty-five tons.

9. Greville Bathe and Dorothy Bathe, *Oliver Evans: A Chronicle of Early American Engineering*, p. 217. This information was taken from a letter written by George Evans to his father, Oliver Evans, in 1814. It was his contention that Daniel French and several other steam-engine manufacturers were violating Oliver Evans's patent on high-pressure steamboat engines.

10. Hall, *Statistics of the West*, p. 231.

11. Marestier, *Memoir on Steamboats*, p. 59.

12. Edwin A. Davis and John C. L. Andreassen, "From Louisville to New Orleans in 1816 Diary of William Newton Mercer," *Journal of Southern History* 2 (Aug., 1939): 394.

13. Charles Cist, *The Cincinnati Miscellany*, p. 152; Morrison, *History of American Steam Navigation*, p. 207; Marestier, *Memoir on Steamboats*, p. 59; Bathe and Bathe, *Oliver Evans*, p. 240. Some sources credit *Washington* as the first vessel to have a horizontal cylinder, to employ flues in the boiler, and to have a cam cutoff. See Morrison, *History of American Steam Navigation*, p. 207. Primary historic data indicates that Shreve did not invent either of these last two devices. Stephen Long claimed to have invented the cam cutoff. Walworth, *The Wheeling Bridge Case*, p. 550. Oliver Evans's description of an engine in 1792 describes a boiler with a flue. Bathe and Bathe, *Oliver Evans*, p. 34.

14. House, *List of Accidents*, p. 15; Gould, *Fifty Years*, p. 107; Hall, *Statistics of the West*, p. 234; James Flint, *Letters from America*, p. 237–38.

15. Hall, *Report on the Ship-Building Industry*, p. 176; Hall, *The West*, p. 157; Gould, *Fifty Years*, p. 108; House, *List of Accidents*, p. 14.

16. Gould, *Fifty Years*, pp. 108–109; Hall, *Statistics of the West*, p. 234; Hall, *Report on the Ship-Building Industry*, p. 176; William J. Petersen, *Steamboating on*

*the Upper Mississippi,* pp. 81–89; Mark W. Kelley, "The Yellowstone Expedition: The American Military on the Missouri River 1818–1820—A Tale of Politics, Personalities, and Pettiness," *Journal of America's Military Past* 27 (Spring/Summer, 2000): 30; Walworth, *The Wheeling Bridge Case,* p. 550 (testimony of Stephen Long); Stephen H. Long, "Explosions of Steam Boilers," *Journal of the Franklin Institute* 8 (Oct., 1831): 244; Edwin James, *Account of an Expedition from Pittsburgh to the Rocky Mountains Performed in the Years 1819, 1820; from the Notes of Major Long, Mr. T. Say and Other Gentlemen,* p. 77.

17. This feature can be seen in the sketch, but Stephen Long also alludes to this arrangement: "The flues extended backward from the fires places quite to the aft end of the boilers, where they united under the center boiler, and were returned through a single flue, to the front, and thence ascended through the deck of the boat, passing upward in a chimney about 19 feet high." Long, "Explosions of Steam Boilers," p. 244.

18. Larry Murphy and Allen R. Saltus, *Phase II Identification and Evaluation of Submerged Cultural Resources in the Tombigbee River Multi-Resource District, Alabama and Mississippi,* p. 161; House, *Report of the Board of Engineers,* p. 22. The idea for a snag chamber may have been first suggested in 1818 by Thomas Hulme: "I would make a partition of strong plank; put it in the broadest fore-part of the boat, right across, and put good iron bolts under the bottom of the boat, through these planks, and screw them on the top of the deck. Then put an upright post in the inside of the boat against the middle of the plank partition and put a spur to the upright post. The partition should be water-tight." *Hulme's Journal of a Tour in the Western Countries of America—September 30, 1818–August 8, 1819,* pp. 78–79.

19. Writing in 1826, B. Drake and E. D. Mansfield noted "the Figure Heads and other sculptured ornament, with which our steamboat are decorated." This indicates that even into the mid-1820s, figureheads were still common on western river steamboats. *Cincinnati in 1826,* p. 73.

20. Hunter, *Steamboats on the Western Rivers,* p. 72.

## Chapter 4

1. James Hall, *Address before the Young Men's Mercantile Library Association, of Cincinnati, in Celebration of Its Eleventh Anniversary, April 18, 1846,* p. 16.

2. In 1880 Henry Hall estimated that the Marine Railway and Dry Dock Company in Cincinnati, Ohio, wasted fully one-half of the wood used in constructing steamboats. *Report on the Ship-Building Industry,* pp. 174, 190, 243. See also Walworth, *The Wheeling Bridge Case,* p. xxix.

3. These figures are based on Hunter, *Steamboats on the Western Rivers,* p. 74, table 4.

4. Henry Howe, *Memoirs of the Most Eminent American Mechanics,* p. 417; Thomas Tredgold, *The Principles and Practice and Explanation of the Machinery Used in Steam Navigation, Volume II, Part I,* p. 39; Ward, "Shallow-Draught River

Steamers," p. 79. See Donald Jackson, *Voyages of the Steamboat* Yellowstone, pp. 160–62; and J. Howard, "Howard and Company Record Book."

5. Hunter, *Steamboats on the Western Rivers*, p. 68; Walworth, *The Wheeling Bridge Case*, p. 442.

6. Jackson, *Voyages of the Steamboat* Yellowstone, p. 160 (excerpt from the contract for the building of *Yellowstone*).

7. Hunter, *Steamboats on the Western Rivers*, pp. 89–90.

8. Walworth, *The Wheeling Bridge Case*, p. 80; William Ferguson, *America by River and Rail*, p. 283; Arese, *Trip to the Prairies*, p. 52.

9. Duden, *Report on a Journey*, p. 192; Gerstner, "Letters from the United States," p. 77; Stevenson, *Civil Engineering of North America*, pp. 152–53.

10. Marestier, *Memoir on Steamboats*, pp. 8–9, 34, 58; Hall, *The West*, p. 160.

11. Walworth, *The Wheeling Bridge Case*, p. 89.

12. Ibid., p. 442 (testimony of Prof. John Locke); Norman S. Russell, "On American River Steamers," *Transactions of the Institution of Naval Architects* 2 (1861): 123–24.

13. Russell, "On American River Steamers," pp. 123–24.

14. William H. Bryan, "The Western River Steamboat," *Transactions of the American Society of Mechanical Engineers* 17 (1896): 395; Prudy, *Report on Steam Navigation*, p. 39. For more information on the effect of silt on steamboat engines, see Thomas Nichols, *Forty Years of American Life, Volume II*, p. 5; and Walworth, *The Wheeling Bridge Case*, p. xxvii.

15. Walworth, *The Wheeling Bridge Case*, p. 224. For discussions regarding the adoption of the high-pressure engine on the western rivers, see Harlan I. Halsey, "The Choice between High-Pressure and Low-Pressure Steam Power in America in the Early Nineteenth Century," *Journal of Economic History* 41 (1981): 740; W. Kemble, "Steam Navigation," *Journal of the Franklin Institute* 11 (Apr., 1846): 227; William Littlefield, "Explosions of Steam Boilers," *Journal of the Franklin Institute* 8 (Nov., 1831): 309–10; Prudy, *Report on Steam Navigation*, p. 39; James Renwick, "Steam Navigation," *Journal of the Franklin Institute* 11 (Apr., 1846): 226; Stevenson, *Civil Engineering of North America*, p. 155; and Walworth, *The Wheeling Bridge Case*, pp. 442, 541.

16. J. V. Merrick, "On the Steamboats of the Western Waters of the United States," *Journal of the Franklin Institute* 23 (May, 1852): 344.

17. U.S. House of Representatives, *Steam Engines*, pp. 321–24. Water's information is based on statistics recorded for the construction of steamboats in Louisville, Kentucky, between 1819 and 1838.

18. Oliver Evans, *The Abortion of the Young Steam Engineer's Guide*, pp. 22–23.

19. Hunter, *Steamboats on the Western Rivers*, p. 153; J. S. Williams, "Propositions and Suggestions on the Means of Obviating or Lessening the Accidents Incident to Navigation by Steam," *Journal of the Franklin Institute* 8 (Nov., 1831): 289; House, *Steam Engines*, pp. 321–24.

20. Littlefield, "Explosions of Steam Boilers," p. 309; Charles Fox, John

Locke, Thomas J. Matthews, Joseph Pierce, and J. Strader, *Report on the Committee Appointed by the Citizens of Cincinnati, April 26, 1838, to Enquire into the Causes of the Explosion of the* Moselle, p. 24; U.S. House of Representatives, *Steamboats,* p. 43; Cadwallader Evans, *A Statement of Experiments upon the Temperature of Steam, the Operations of the Common Safety Valve, and upon Government Alloys,* p. 33.

21. Fox et al., *Report on the Explosion of the* Moselle, p. 58; U.S. House of Representatives, *Relative to Steamboat Explosions,* p. 10.

22. Erasmus W. Benton, "Explosions of Steam Boilers," *Journal of the Franklin Institute* 8 (Nov., 1831): 312–13; U.S. Senate, *Mr. Cist's Second Communication,* p. 66; Thomas J. Halderman, "Explosions of Steam Boilers," *Journal of the Franklin Institute* 9 (Jan., 1832): 30; House, *Relative to Steamboat Explosions,* p. 10; Williams, "Lessening the Accidents Incident to Navigation by Steam," p. 289; U.S. Senate, *Report of the Commissioner of Patents, to the Senate of the United States, on the Subject of Steam Boiler Explosions,* p. 12; Thomas Cooper, Joseph Cloud, Jacob Perkins, and Frederick Graff, "Explosions of Steam Boilers," *Journal of the Franklin Institute* 8 (Oct., 1831): 239.

23. Walworth, *The Wheeling Bridge Case,* pp. 399, 413, 419.

24. Ibid., pp. 80, 419; Thomas W. Bakewell, "Explosions of Steam Boilers," *Journal of the Franklin Institute* 8 (Dec., 1831): 385; Matthew Robinson, "Explosions of Steam Boilers," *Journal of the Franklin Institute* 8 (Nov., 1831): 311; Senate, *Report of the Commissioner of Patents,* p. 11.

25. Thomas W. Bakewell, "Explosion of the Steamer *Redstone,*" *Journal of the Franklin Institute* 23 (June, 1852): 413; Fox et al., *Report on the Explosion of the* Moselle, p. 23; A. C. Jones, "An Account of the Explosion of the Steamboat *Brilliant,*" *Journal of the Franklin Institute* 23 (May, 1852): 324.

26. Gauge cocks were also known as try cocks.

27. George B. Merrick, *Old Times on the Upper Mississippi: The Recollections of a Steamboat Pilot from 1854 to 1863,* p. 39; Senate, *Report of the Commissioner of Patents,* p. 20; Fox et al., *Report on the Explosion of the* Moselle, pp. 34, 40–41.

28. Benton, "Explosions of Steam Boilers," pp. 313–14; Halderman, "Explosions of Steam Boilers," p. 30; Jacob Perkins, "Remarks on the Explosion of Steam Boilers," *Journal of the Franklin Institute* 9 (May, 1832): 346; U.S. Senate, *No. 6,* 26th Cong., 2d sess., 1841, S. Doc. 378, p. 178. See also John L. Sullivan, "On the Safety of Steam Boats," *Journal of the Franklin Institute* 6 (Nov., 1830): 355–56.

29. Alan Bates, *The Western Rivers Engineroom Cyclopoedium,* p. 18; David Prentice, "Letter from the Secretary of the Treasury Transmitting Information Collected by the Department, upon the Subject of Accidents on Board of Steam Boats," in House, *List of Accidents,* p. 16; Halderman, "Explosions of Steam Boilers," p. 30; Walworth, *The Wheeling Bridge Case,* p. 72; Alan Bates, personal communication with author, Dec., 2002; John G. Cassedy, "Explosions of Steam Boilers," *Journal of the Franklin Institute* 9 (Feb., 1832): 95; Fox

et al., *Report on the Explosion of the* Moselle, p. 41; House, *Relative to Steamboat Explosions,* p. 20.

30. Hunter, *Steamboats on the Western Rivers,* p. 163; Gilman, "Steamboats on the Western Waters," p. 210.

31. Senate, *Report of the Commissioner of Patents,* p. 20; Stevenson, *Civil Engineering of North America,* pp. 157, 164–65; U.S. Senate, *No. 13,* pp. 66–67.

32. Benton, "Explosions of Steam Boilers," p. 314; Bates, *Western Rivers Engineroom Cyclopoedium,* p. 10.

33. Stevenson, *Civil Engineering of North America,* p. 152. This positioning also served to announce the approach of the vessel at night.

34. Walworth, *The Wheeling Bridge Case,* pp. 89, 635–39 (table of measurements of steamboats compiled by Israel Dickenson).

35. Stevenson, *Civil Engineering of North America,* p. 156; International Correspondence Schools, *The Machinery of Western River Steamboats,* p. 60. The breeching was also commonly referred to as the britching.

36. Bates, *Western Rivers Engineroom Cyclopoeduim,* p. 11; Stevenson, *Civil Engineering of North America,* p. 156; Walworth, *The Wheeling Bridge Case,* p. 452.

37. Walworth, *The Wheeling Bridge Case,* p. 572.

38. Senate, *Mr. Cist's Second Communication,* p. 69; Walworth, *The Wheeling Bridge Case,* p. xxvii.

39. Merrick, *Old Times on the Upper Mississippi,* p. 37.

40. Alan Bates, "Paddlewheel Efficiency," *Egregious Steamboat Journal* 22 (1994): 11.

41. Ibid., p. 12.

42. Walworth, *The Wheeling Bridge Case,* p. 521.

43. Ibid., pp. 389, 407–408, 419.

44. Ibid., p. 633.

### Chapter 5

1. Bryan, "Western River Steamboat," p. 393; Howe, *Memoirs of the Most Eminent American Mechanics,* p. 417; Hunter, *Steamboats on the Western Rivers,* p. 121; Tredgold, *Machinery Used in Steam Navigation, Volume II, Part I,* p. 39.

2. James S. Buckingham, *The Eastern and Western States of America, Volume II,* p. 167. Charles Lyell, traveling on a stern-wheeler in 1842, recorded afterward: "We embarked . . . in a long narrow steamer, which drew only eighteen inches water, and had a single paddle behind like the overshot wheel of a mill. It threw up a shower of spray like a fountain, which had a picturesque effect." Lyell, *Travels in North America; with Geological Observations on the United States, Canada & Nova Scotia,* p. 30.

3. Walworth, *The Wheeling Bridge Case,* pp. xxvii, 184, 406, 411. See also Scott Russell, "On the Progress of Naval Architecture and Steam Navigation," *Journal of the Franklin Institute* 24 (Mar., 1855): 196–97.

4. Hall, *Report on the Ship-Building Industry,* pp. 175, 176; Alan Bates, per-

sonal communication with author, Dec., 2002; Tredgold, *Machinery Used in Steam Navigation, Volume II, Part I*, p. 38.

5. Jack Custer, "Types of Steamboat Bows," *Egregious Steamboat Journal* 9 (1992): 17–28.

6. Ibid., p. 27.

7. Bert L. Baldwin, "Pittsburg [*sic*] and Cincinnati Packet Line Stern Wheel Steamer *Queen City*," *Marine Engineering* 1 (1897): 6.

8. Hunter, *Steamboats on the Western Rivers*, p. 91.

9. Ibid., p. 90. Traveling on a steamboat in 1849, Robert Baird noted: "These steamers vary somewhat in construction, as they do in size and in elegance; and some of them have even an additional deck or 'flat' [the Texas], to those above mentioned." Baird, *Impressions and Experiences of the West Indies and North America in 1849*, p. 16.

10. John M. Sweeney, "River Practice of the West," *Transactions of the American Society of Mechanical Engineers* 9 (1887–88): 645; Jack Custer, "Hogchains: Their Whys and Wherefores," *Egregious Steamboat Journal* 2 (1991): 12.

11. Hunter, *Steamboats on the Western Rivers*, p. 96. The average length-to-depth ratio for vessels of 400–500 tons increased from 15:1 to 27:1 between 1827 and 1841.

12. Russell, "On American River Steamers," p. 123.

13. Bates, *Western Rivers Steamboat Cyclopoedium*, p. 28; Russell, "On American River Steamers," pp. 112–13.

14. See Stewart-Abernathy, *Ghost Boats*, pp. 79–92; and Pearson and Saltus, *Underwater Archaeology on the Ouachita River*, p. 76.

15. Department of the Navy, *Wood: A Manual for Its Use as a Shipbuilding Material*, pp. 13, 16; Hall, *Report on the Ship-Building Industry*, p. 245. On the use of other woods in steamboat construction, see Goodwin et al., "Archeological Investigations of the Shipwreck *Kentucky*," p. 262; Pearson and Birchett, *History and Archaeology of Two Civil War Steamboats*, p. 227; and Howard, "Howard and Company Record Book."

16. Hunter, *Steamboats on the Western Rivers*, p. 78.

17. The keel of a western river steamboat was also known as the king plank.

18. James et al., *Evaluations of Sites 22Lf966, 22Lf967, and 22Lf969*, pp. 148–55.

19. Howard, "Howard and Company Record Book," pp. 10, 129.

20. John C. Howard, "Reminiscences by John C. Howard Rafting and Timbering," Howard Ship Yard and Dock Company Collection, Lilly Library, Indiana University, Bloomington.

21. Russell, "On American River Steamers," p. 122; Howard, "Howard and Company Record Book," p. 54.

22. Goodwin et al., "Archeological Investigations of the Shipwreck *Kentucky*," pp. 266–67.

23. Streaks were also commonly known as stringers or strakes. The selec-

tion of the term "streak" is based on the language used by the Howard Ship Yard and Dock Company as reflected in Howard, "Howard and Company Record Book."

24. Pearson and Birchett, *History and Archaeology of Two Civil War Steamboats*, p. 190.

25. Pearson, "Underwater Archaeology along the Lower Pearl River," p. 74.

26. William C. Redfield, "Correspondence with the United States Board of Navy Commissioner," *Journal of the Franklin Institute* 12 (July, 1846): 10; Andrew Murray and Robert Murray, *Ship-Building in Iron and Wood, by Andrew Murray and Steam-Ships, by Robert Murray*, p. 87.

27. Goodwin et al, "Archeological Investigations of the Shipwreck *Kentucky*," pp. 277–78; James et al., *Evaluations of Sites 22Lf966, 22Lf967, and 22Lf969*, pp. 169–70.

28. Russell, "On American River Steamers," p. 122.

29. Hunter, *Steamboats on the Western Rivers*, p. 93.

30. Howard, "Howard and Company Record Book," pp. 10–11.

31. Walworth, *The Wheeling Bridge Case*, pp. 635–39 (table of measurements of steamboats compiled by Israel Dickenson). For another good depiction of boilers on mid-nineteenth-century steamboats, see B. H. Bartol, *A Treatise on the Marine Boilers of the United States*, pp. 139–40.

32. Walworth, *The Wheeling Bridge Case*, p. 453 (testimony of Prof. John Locke).

33. T. M. Rees, "The Development of Western River Steamboats," *International Marine Engineering* 14 (Sept., 1909): 344, 345; International Correspondence Schools, *Machinery of Western River Steamboats*, p. 55; Walworth, *The Wheeling Bridge Case*, p. 49 (testimony of Jacob Hazlep, a steamboat pilot); Frederick D. Herbert, "Steamboating on the Mississippi," *International Marine Engineering* 12 (May, 1907): 188. The testimony of William Stewart, a steamboat builder, indicates that the doctor was in common use by 1850 in the largest class of packet boats on the Ohio River. But there were more small steamboats that did not use it than those that did. Walworth, *The Wheeling Bridge Case*, p. 531.

34. Rees, "Development of Western River Steamboats," p. 344; International Correspondence Schools, *Machinery of Western River Steamboats*, pp. 55–57.

35. Walworth, *The Wheeling Bridge Case*, pp. 58, 60, 69, 445, 530.

36. Ibid., pp. 57, 58, 71, 73, 445.

37. Ibid., pp. 419, 520, 571.

38. Ibid., pp. 66, 87, 415, 541.

39. P. R. Hodge, *The Steam Engine, Its Origin and Gradual Improvement*, p. 125; Walworth, *The Wheeling Bridge Case*, p. 413.

40. Merrick, "Steamboats of the Western Waters," p. 344. David Stevenson noted in 1838 that both one- and two-engine boats were in existence. Stevenson, *Civil Engineering of North America*, p. 153.

41. Gilman, "Steamboats on the Western Waters," p. 209; Walworth, *The Wheeling Bridge Case*, pp. 636–39 (table of measurements of steamboats compiled by Israel Dickenson).

42. Ward, "Shallow-Draught River Steamers," p. 85; Bryan, "Western River Steamboat," p. 394; Pearson and Saltus, *Underwater Archaeology on the Ouachita River,* pp. 70–74.

43. House, *Steam Engines*, pp. 321–24; Hunter, *Steamboats on the Western Rivers,* p. 143.

44. "Poppet valve" and "puppet valve" both appear frequently in the literature.

45. Ward, "Shallow-Draught River Steamers," p. 85; Bates, *Western Rivers Engineroom Cyclopoedium*, p. 39.

46. Russell, "On American River Steamers," p. 125.

47. Merrick, *Old Times on the Upper Mississippi*, pp. 41–42; Ward, "Shallow-Draught River Steamers," p. 85.

48. Bates, *Western Rivers Engineroom Cyclopoedium*, p. 39.

49. Russell, "On American River Steamers," p. 124; Bryan, "Western River Steamboat," p. 395. The length of the pitman was in proportion to the length of the stroke. In 1840 the pitman was three and one-half times the stroke. Hodge, *Steam Engine*, p. 240.

50. Tredgold, *Machinery Used in Steam Navigation, Volume II, Part I*, p. 40; Samuel H. Gilman, "Steamboats in the Western Waters," *Journal of the Franklin Institute* 25 (Apr., 1853): 259; Hodge, *Steam Engine*, p. 125.

51. Tredgold, *Machinery Used in Steam Navigation, Volume II, Part I*, p. 41.

52. Walworth, *The Wheeling Bridge Case*, pp. 88–89, 403, 426, 532.

53. Bates, *Western Rivers Steamboat Cyclopoedium*, p. 93.

# BIBLIOGRAPHY

Adams, Henry C. *Report on the Transportation Business in the United States at the Eleventh Census: 1890. Part II—Transportation by Water.* Washington, D.C.: Government Printing Office, 1894.

Adams, R. M. *The Black Cloud Survey.* College Station: Texas A&M University, 1978.

Allen, M. *Western Rivermen, 1763–1861: Ohio and Mississippi Boatmen and the Myth of the Alligator Horse.* Baton Rouge: Louisiana State University Press, 1990.

Allen, Thomas; A. B. Chambers; N. J. Eaton; George K. McGunnegle; Wilson Primm; Samuel Treat; and James E. Yeatman. *The Commerce and Navigation of the Valley of the Mississippi; and also That Appertaining to the City of St. Louis: Considered, with Reference to the Improvement, by the General Government, of the Mississippi River and Its Principal Tributaries.* St. Louis: Chamber and Knapp, 1847.

Andrist, Ralph K., and C. Bradford Mitchell. *Steamboats on the Mississippi.* New York: American Heritage, 1962.

Anonymous. "Steamboats on the Western Waters." *Journal of the Franklin Institute* 14 (November, 1834): 353–56.

Appleby, Joyce O. *Capitalism and a New Social Order: The Republican Vision of the 1790s.* New York: New York University Press, 1984.

Arese, Francesco. *A Trip to the Prairies and the Interior of North America (1837–1838).* New York: Cooper Square, 1975.

Arfwedson, Carl David. *The United State and Canada in 1832, 1833, and 1834.* New York: Johnson Reprint, 1969.

Armroyd, George. *A Connected View of the Whole Internal Navigation of the United States.* Philadelphia: Lydia R. Bailey, 1830.

Atack, Jeremy; Fred Bateman; and Thomas Weiss. "The Regional Diffusion and Adoption of the Steam Engine in American Manufacturing." *Journal of Economic History* 40 (June, 1980): 281–308.

Baird, Robert. *Impressions and Experiences of the West Indies and North America in 1849.* Edinburgh: William Blackwood and Sons, 1850.

Bakewell, Thomas W. "Explosions of Steam Boilers." *Journal of the Franklin Institute* 8 (December, 1831): 382–88.

———. "Explosion of the Steamer *Redstone.*" *Journal of the Franklin Institute* 23 (June, 1852): 413–14.

Baldwin, Bert L. "Pittsburg [*sic*] and Cincinnati Packet Line Stern Wheel Steamer *Queen City.*" *Marine Engineering* 1 (1897): 5–11.

Baldwin, Leland D. "Shipbuilding on the Western Waters, 1793–1817." *The Mississippi Valley Historical Review* 20 (June, 1933): 29–44.
———. *The Keelboat Age on Western Waters.* Pittsburgh: University of Pittsburgh Press, 1941.
Bartol, B. H. *A Treatise on the Marine Boilers of the United States.* Philadelphia: R. W. Barnard and Sons, 1851.
Bates, Alan L. *The Western Rivers Steamboat Cyclopoedium; or American Riverboat Structure & Detail, Salted with Lore.* Leonia, N.J.: Hustle, 1968.
———. "Paddlewheel Efficiency." *Egregious Steamboat Journal* 22 (1994): 11–13.
———. *The Western Rivers Engineroom Cyclopoedium.* Louisville: Cyclopoedium, 1996.
Bathe, Greville, and Dorothy Bathe. *Oliver Evans: A Chronicle of Early American Engineering.* New York: Arno, 1972.
Benton, Erasmus W. "Explosions of Steam Boilers." *Journal of the Franklin Institute* 8 (November, 1831): 306–15.
Bolles, Albert S. *Industrial History of the United States,* Norwich, Conn.: Henry Bill, 1881.
Bryan, William H. "The Western River Steamboat." *Transactions of the American Society of Mechanical Engineers* 17 (1896): 386–97.
Buckingham, James S. *The Eastern and Western States of America, Volume II.* London: Fisher, Son, 1842.
Buttrick, Tilly. *Voyages, Travels & Discoveries of Tilly Buttrick, Jr.* Boston: John Putnam: 1831.
Callender, G. S. "The Early Transportation and Banking Enterprises of the States in Relation to the Growth of Corporations." *Quarterly Journal of Economics* 17 (November, 1902): 111–62.
Cassedy, John G. "Explosions of Steam Boilers." *Journal of the Franklin Institute* 9 (February, 1832): 94–99.
Cist, Charles. *The Cincinnati Miscellany.* New York: Arno, 1971.
Cooper, Thomas; Joseph Cloud; Jacob Perkins; and Frederick Graff. "Explosions of Steam Boilers." *Journal of the Franklin Institute* 8 (October, 1831): 237–39.
Corbin, Annalies. "Shifting Sand and Muddy Water: Historic Cartography and River Migration as Factors in Locating Steamboat Wrecks on the Far Upper Missouri River." *Historical Archaeology* 32, no. 4 (1998): 86–94.
———. *The Material Culture of Steamboat Passengers: Archaeological Evidence from the Missouri River.* New York: Kluwer Academic/Plenum, 1999.
Custer, Jack. "Hogchains: Their Whys and Wherefores." *Egregious Steamboat Journal* 2 (1991): 10–15, 36.
———. "Types of Steamboat Bows." *Egregious Steamboat Journal* 9 (1992): 17–28.
———. "The Sternwheel." *Egregious Steamboat Journal* 14 (1993): 17–27.

————. "Building a Steamboat." *Egregious Steamboat Journal* 31 (1997):17–26.

Davis, Edwin A., and John C. L. Andreassen. "From Louisville to New Orleans in 1816 Diary of William Newton Mercer." *Journal of Southern History* 2 (August, 1939): 390–402.

Department of Navy. *Wood: A Manual for Its Use as a Shipbuilding Material.* Kingston, Mass.: Teaparty, 1983.

Dickens, Charles. *American Notes.* London: Oxford University Press, 1850.

Drake, B., and E. D. Mansfield. *Cincinnati in 1826.* Cincinnati: Morgan, Lodge, and Fisher, 1827.

Duden, Gottfried. *Report on a Journey to the Western States of North America (during the Years 1824, '25, '26, and 1827).* Columbia: State Historical Society of Missouri and University of Missouri Press, 1980.

Dunbar, Seymor. *A History of Travel in America, Being an Outline of the Development in Modes of Travel from Archaic Vehicles of Colonial Times to the Completion of the First Transcontinental Railroad.* New York: Tudor, 1937.

Ellis, R. E. "The Political Economy of Thomas Jefferson." In *Thomas Jefferson: The Man, His World, His Influence,* edited by Lally Weymouth, 81–95. London: Weidenfeld & Nicolson, 1973.

Evans, Cadwallader. *A Statement of Experiments upon the Temperature of Steam, the Operations of the Common Safety Valve, and upon Government Alloys.* Pittsburgh: Keenan & Hopkins, 1854.

Evans, Oliver. *The Abortion of the Young Steam Engineer's Guide.* Philadelphia: Fry and Kammerer, 1805.

Ferguson, William. *America by River and Rail.* London: James Nisbet, 1856.

Flint, James. *Letters from America.* London: W&C Tait, 1822.

Foreman, Grant. "River Navigation in the Early Southwest." *The Mississippi Valley Historical Review* 15 (June, 1928): 34–55.

Fox, Charles; John Locke; Thomas J. Matthews; Joseph Pierce; and J. Strader. *Report on the Committee Appointed by the Citizens of Cincinnati, April 26, 1838, to Enquire into the Causes of the Explosion of the* Moselle. Cincinnati: Alexander Flash, 1838.

Gandy, Joan W., and Thomas H. Gandy. *The Mississippi Steamboat Era in Historic Photographs: Natchez to New Orleans 1870 to 1920.* New York: Dover, 1987.

Gearhart, Robert L., and Steven D. Hoyt. *Channel to Liberty: Underwater Archaeological Investigations, Liberty County, Texas.* Austin: Espey, Huston, and Associates, 1990.

Gephart, William F. *Transportation and Industrial Development in the Middle West.* New York: Octagon, 1976.

Gerstner, Francis Anthony Chevalier de. "Letters from the United States of North America on Internal Improvements, Steam Navigation, Banking, &c." *Journal of the Franklin Institute* 1 (February, 1841): 73–83.

Gilman, Samuel H. "Steamboats on the Western Waters." *Journal of the Franklin Institute* 24 (September, 1852): 207–11.

———. "Steamboats in the Western Waters." *Journal of the Franklin Institute* 25 (April, 1853): 258–63.

Goodwin, R. Christopher; John L. Seidel; David S. Robinson; Adam I. Kane; and Martha R. Williams. *Phase II and III Archeological Investigations of the Shipwreck* Kentucky *(Site 16BO358) at Eagle Bend, Pool 5, Red River Waterway, Bossier Parish, Louisiana.* Frederick, Md.: R. Christopher Goodwin and Associates, 2000. Draft report.

Gould, Emerson W. *Fifty Years on the Mississippi; or Gould's History of River Navigation.* St. Louis: Nixon-Jones, 1889.

Haites, Erick F. *Ohio and Mississippi River Transportation, 1810–1860.* West Lafayette, Ind.: Purdue University, 1969.

Haites, Erick F., and James Mak. "The Decline of Steamboating on the Antebellum Western Rivers: Some New Evidence and an Alternative Hypothesis." *Explorations in Economic History* 11 (Fall, 1973): 25–36.

———. "Social Savings Due to Western River Steamboats." *Research in Economic History* 3 (1978): 263–304.

Haites, Erick F.; James Mak; and G. M. Walton. *Western River Transportation: The Era of Early Internal Development, 1810–1860.* Baltimore: Johns Hopkins University Press, 1975.

Halderman, Thomas J. "Explosions of Steam Boilers." *Journal of the Franklin Institute* 9 (January, 1832): 24–30.

Hall, Henry. *Report on the Ship-Building Industry of the United States.* New York: Library Editions, 1970.

Hall, James. *Sketches of History, Life, and Manners, in the West, Volume II.* Philadelphia: Harrison Hall, 1835.

———. *Statistics of the West at the Close of the Year 1836.* Cincinnati: J. A. James, 1837.

———. *Address before the Young Men's Mercantile Library Association, of Cincinnati, in Celebration of Its Eleventh Anniversary, April 18, 1846.* Cincinnati: Associates, 1846.

———. *The West: Its Commerce and Navigation.* Cincinnati: H. W. Derby, 1848.

Halsey, Harlan I. "The Choice between High-Pressure and Low-Pressure Steam Power in America in the Early Nineteenth Century." *Journal of Economic History* 41 (December, 1981): 723–44.

Handlin, O., and M. F. Handlin. *Commonwealth: A Study of the Role of Government in the American Economy: Massachusetts. 1774–1861.* 2d ed. Cambridge: Belknap Press of Harvard University Press, 1969.

Harris, Isaac. *Harris' Pittsburgh Business Directory for the Year 1837.* Pittsburgh: Isaac Harris, 1837.

Hawley, Greg. *Treasure in a Cornfield: The Discovery and Excavation of the Steamboat* Arabia. Kansas City, Mo.: Paddle Wheel, 1998.

Hedrick, David L. *The Investigation of the Caney Creek Shipwreck Archaeological Site 41MG32.* College Station: Texas A&M University, 1998.

Herbert, Frederick D. "Steamboating on the Mississippi." *International Marine Engineering* 12 (May, 1907): 186–90.

Hilton, George W.; R. Plummer; Joseph Jobe; and Carlo Demand. *The Illustrated History of Paddle Steamers.* New York: Two Continents, 1976.

Hoagland, H. E. "Early Transportation on the Mississippi." *The Journal of Political Economy* 19 (February, 1911): 111–23.

Hodge, P. R. *The Steam Engine, Its Origin and Gradual Improvement.* New York: D. Appleton, 1840.

U.S. Senate. *No. 13.* 31st Cong., spec. sess., 1849. S. Doc. 547, pp. 66–68.

Howard, J. "Howard and Company Record Book." 1877–87. Collection of the Howard Steamboat Museum, Jeffersonville, Ind.

Howe, Henry. *Memoirs of the Most Eminent American Mechanics.* New York: Alexander V. Blake, 1844.

Hulme, Thomas. *Hulme's Journal of a Tour in the Western Countries of America— September 30, 1818–August 8, 1819.* Cleveland, Ohio, 1904.

Hunter, Louis C. *Steamboats on the Western Rivers: An Economic and Technological History.* New York: Dover, 1993.

International Correspondence Schools. *The Machinery of Western River Steamboats.* Scranton, Pa.: Colliery Engineer, 1900.

Irion, Jack. *Archaeological Testing of the Confederate Obstructions, 1Mb28, Mobile Harbor, Alabama.* Austin: Espey, Huston, and Associates, 1985.

Jackson, Donald. *Voyages of the Steamboat Yellowstone.* New York: Ticknor and Fields, 1985.

James, Edwin. *Account of an Expedition from Pittsburgh to the Rocky Mountains Performed in the Years 1819, 1820; from the Notes of Major Long, Mr. T. Say and Other Gentlemen.* London: Longman, Hurst, Rees, Orme, and Brown, 1823.

James, Steven R., and Charles E. Pearson. *Submerged Cultural Resources Investigations of the Steamboat J. D. Hinde (41LB85), Channel to Liberty, Liberty County, Texas.* Baton Rouge: Coastal Environments, 1993.

James, Steven R., Michael C. Krivor, Alan Whitehead, Kristen Zoelmer, and Michael C. Tuttle, *National Register of Historic Places Eligibility Evaluations of Sites 22Lf966, 22Lf967, and 22Lf969, Limited Survey, and National Register of Historic Places Eligibility Evaluations of All Bridges, Structures, and Revisited Targets Located within Items 3 and 4 of the Upper Yazoo Projects, Yazoo River, Leflore County, Mississippi.* Memphis: Panamerican Consultants, 2002.

Jones, A. C. "An Account of the Explosion of the Steamboat *Brilliant.*" *Journal of the Franklin Institute* 23 (May, 1852): 322–24.

Kane, Adam I.; Jean B. Pelletier; Martha Williams; David S. Robinson; and Roger Saucier. *A Cultural Resources Survey of Items 3B-2 and 4 of the Upper Yazoo River Projects, Leflore County, Mississippi.* Frederick, Md.: R. Christopher Goodwin and Associates, 1998.

Kelley, Mark W. "The Yellowstone Expedition: The American Military on the Missouri River, 1818–1820—A Tale of Politics, Personalities, and Pettiness." *Journal of America's Military Past* 27 (Spring/Summer, 2000): 17–53.

Kemble, W. "Steam Navigation." *Journal of the Franklin Institute* 11 (April, 1846): 225–36.

Kloppe, C. B., Andrew W. Hall, and Joe J. Simmons, *The* A. S. Ruthven. Austin: Southwest Underwater Archaeological Society and Texas Historical Commission, 1998.

Lanman, J. H. "American Steam Navigation." *Hunt's Merchants' Magazine* 4 (1841): 120–21, 123–24.

Latrobe, J. *The First Steamboat Voyage on the Western Waters*. Baltimore, 1871.

Law, John; C. I. Battell; Hamilton Smith; Elisha Embree; Isaac Hutchinson; John Ingle; and M. J. Bray. "Memorial from a Meeting of Citizens of the West, Held at Evansville Indiana, on the Subject of Western Interests." *House Documents* 31st Cong., 2d sess., 3 (1850): 1–12.

Lees, William B., and J. Barto Arnold III. "Preliminary Assessment of a Wreck in the Red River, Choctaw County, Oklahoma, USA." *The International Journal of Nautical Archaeology* 29, no. 1 (2000): 120–25.

Lippincott, Isaac. " Pioneer Industry in the West." *The Journal of Political Economy* 18 (April, 1910): 269–93.

———. *A History of Manufactures in the Ohio Valley to the Year 1860*. New York: Knickerbocker, 1914.

Littlefield, William. "Explosions of Steam Boilers." *Journal of the Franklin Institute* 8 (November, 1831): 308–10.

Long, Stephen H. "Explosions of Steam Boilers." *Journal of the Franklin Institute* 8 (October, 1831): 234–47.

———. "Extent of Steam Navigation on the Western Waters, Including the Rivers, Bayous, &c., Connected with the Mississippi by Channels Navigable for Steamers." *Journal of the Franklin Institute* 15 (May, 1848): 354–55.

Luffman, John. "A Map of North America." *Geographic Principles*. London: Booth, 1803.

Lyell, Charles. *Travels in North American; with Geological Observations on the United States, Canada & Nova Scotia*. London: John Murray, 1845.

Lyford, William G. *The Western Address Directory*. Baltimore: Joseph Robinson, 1837.

Maass, Alfred R. "Daniel French and the Western Steamboat Engine." *American Neptune* 56 (Winter, 1996): 29–44.

Mackay, Charles. *Life and Liberty in America; or, Sketches of a Tour in the United States and Canada, in 1857–8*. London: Smith, Elder, 1859.

Mak, James, and Gary M. Walton. "Steamboats and the Great Productivity Surge in River Transportation." *Journal of Economic History* 3 (September, 1972): 619–40.

————. "The Persistence of Old Technologies: The Case of Flatboats." *Journal of Economic History* 33 (June, 1973): 444–51.

Marestier, Jean B. *Memoir on Steamboats of the United States of America.* Paris: Royal, 1824.

Martineau, Harriet. *Retrospect of Western Travel.* New York: Greenwood, 1969.

McCoy, Drew R. *The Elusive Republic: Political Economy in Jeffersonian America.* Chapel Hill: University of North Carolina Press, 1980.

Meinig, Donald W. *The Shaping of America: A Geographical Perspective on 500 Years of History, Volume 2, Continental America, 1800–1867.* New Haven: Yale University Press, 1993.

Merrick, George B. *Old Times on the Upper Mississippi: The Recollections of a Steamboat Pilot from 1854 to 1863.* Cleveland: A. H. Clark, 1909.

Merrick, J. V. "On the Steamboats of the Western Waters of the United States." *Journal of the Franklin Institute* 23 (May, 1852): 344–48.

Monroe, Thomas M. *Remarks of Thomas M. Monroe, of Dubuque, Iowa, before the National Board of Trade.* Richmond: Gary, Clemmitt, & Jones, 1869.

Montulé, Edouard de. *Travels in America, 1816–1817.* Bloomington: Indiana University Press, 1951.

Morrison, John H. *History of American Steam Navigation.* New York: Stephen Daye, 1958.

Murphy, Larry, and Allen R. Saltus. *Phase II Identification and Evaluation of Submerged Cultural Resources in the Tombigbee River Multi-Resource District, Alabama and Mississippi.* Montgomery: University of Alabama, 1985.

Murray, Andrew, and Robert Murray. *Ship-Building in Iron and Wood, by Andrew Murray and Steam-Ships, by Robert Murray.* Edinburgh: A. and C. Black, 1863.

Neff, George. *Proceedings of a Meeting of the Citizens of Cincinnati Held at the Council Chamber, January 22, 1846, Expressing the Sense of the Citizens on the Subject of Improving the Navigation around the Falls of the Ohio River.* Cincinnati: Daily Atlas, 1846.

Nichols, Thomas. *Forty Years of American Life, Volume II.* London: John Maxwell, 1864.

North, Douglas C. *The Economic Growth of the United States, 1790–1860.* New York: W. W. Norton, 1966.

Pearson, Charles E. "Underwater Archaeology along the Lower Pearl River, Mississippi and Louisiana." *Mississippi Archaeology* 36 (Winter, 2001).

Pearson, Charles E., and Thomas C. C. Birchett. *The History and Archaeology of Two Civil War Steamboats: The Ironclad Gunboat USS* Eastport *and the Steamer* Ed. F. Dix. Baton Rouge: Coastal Environments, 2001.

Pearson, Charles E., and Allen R. Saltus. *Underwater Archaeology on the Ouachita River, Arkansas: The Search for the* Chieftain, Haydee, *and* Homer. Baton Rouge: Coastal Environments, 1993.

Perkins, Jacob. "Remarks on the Explosion of Steam Boilers." *Journal of the Franklin Institute* 9 (May, 1832): 346–49.

Petersen, William J. *Steamboating on the Upper Mississippi.* New York: Dover, 1995.

Petsche, Jerome E. *The Steamboat Bertrand: History, Excavation, and Architecture.* Washington, D.C.: National Park Service, 1974.

Prudy, T. C. *Report on Steam Navigation in the United States.* Washington, D.C.: Department of the Interior, Census Office, 1890.

Redfield, William C. "Correspondence with the United States Board of Navy Commissioner." *Journal of the Franklin Institute* 12 (July, 1846): 1–18.

Rees, T. M. "The Development of Western River Steamboats." *International Marine Engineering* 14 (September, 1909): 344–48.

Renwick, James. *Treatise on the Steam Engine.* New York: Carvill, 1839.

———. "Steam Navigation." *Journal of the Franklin Institute* 11 (April, 1846): 223–25.

Ringwalt, John L. *Development of Transportation Systems in the United States.* Philadelphia: Published by the author, Railway World Office, 1888.

Robinson, Matthew. "Explosions of Steam Boilers." *Journal of the Franklin Institute* 8 (November, 1831): 310–12.

Russell, Norman S. "On American River Steamers." *Transactions of the Institution of Naval Architects* 2 (1861): 105–27 (plates IX–XIV).

Russell, Scott. "On the Progress of Naval Architecture and Steam Navigation." *Journal of the Franklin Institute* 24 (March, 1855): 196–98.

Saltus, Allen R.; George J. Castille; and Charles E. Pearson. *Natchez under the Hill: Historical and Archaeological Investigation of Watercraft along the Mississippi River, Adams County, Mississippi.* Baton Rouge: Coastal Environments, 1995.

Sellers, Charles G. *The Market Revolution: Jacksonian America, 1815–1846.* New York: Oxford University Press, 1991.

Stevenson, David. *Sketch of the Civil Engineering of North America.* London: John Weale, 1838.

Stewart-Abernathy, Leslie C. *Ghost Boats on the Mississippi: Discovering Our Working Past.* Fayetteville: Arkansas Archeological Survey, 2003.

Sullivan, John L. "On the Safety of Steam Boats." *Journal of the Franklin Institute* 6 (November, 1830): 352–58.

Sweeney, John M. "River Practice of the West." *Transactions of the American Society of Mechanical Engineers* 9 (1887–88): 645–70.

Taylor, George R. *The Transportation Revolution, 1815–1860.* New York: M. E. Sharpe, 1989.

Thomas, David. *Travels through the Western Country in the Summer of 1816.* Hartford, Conn.: Hafner, 1970.

Tredgold, Thomas. *The Principles and Practice and Explanation of the Machinery Used in Steam Navigation, Volume II, Part I.* London: John Weale, 1851.

———. *The Principles and Practice and Explanation of the Machinery Used in Steam Navigation, Volume II, Part II.* London: John Weale, 1851.

U.S. House of Representatives. *Report of the Board of Engineers, on the Ohio and Mississippi Rivers.* 17th Cong., 2d sess., 1822. H. Doc. 35, pp. 7–22.

———. *List of Accidents from Bursting of Boilers, on Board of Steam Boats, upon the Mississippi, and Its Tributaries.* 18th Cong., 2d sess., 1825. H. Doc. 116, pp. 1–21.

———. *Steamboats.* 22d Cong., 1st sess., 1832. H. Doc. 228, pp. 1–87.

———. *Steam Engines.* 25th Cong., 3d sess., 1838. H. Doc. 345, pp. 321–26.

———. *Relative to Steamboat Explosions.* 28th Cong., 1st sess., 1844. H. Doc. 68, pp. 1–21.

U.S. Senate. *Mr. Cist's Second Communication.* 26th Cong., 2d sess., 1841. S. Doc. 378, pp. 59–71.

———. *No. 6.* 26th Cong., 2d sess., 1841. S. Doc. 378, pp. 161–84.

———. *Report of the Commissioner of Patents, to the Senate of the United States, on the Subject of Steam Boiler Explosions.* 30th Cong., 2d sess., 1848. S. Doc. 529, pp. 1–53.

Walworth, R. Hyde. *Order of Reference of the Supreme Court of the United States in the Case of the State of Pennsylvania, Complainant, against the Wheeling & Belmont Bridge Company and Others, Defendants.* Washington, D.C., 1850.

Ward, Charles. "Shallow-Draught River Steamers." *Transactions of the Society of Naval Architects and Marine Engineers* 17 (1909): 79–108, plates 23–86.

White, Samuel. "New, Immense, Unbounded World." *Annals of Congress* 8th Cong., 1st sess. (1804): 33–34.

Williams, J. S. "Propositions and Suggestions on the Means of Obviating or Lessening the Accidents Incident to Navigation by Steam." *Journal of the Franklin Institute* 8 (November, 1831): 289–95.

Way, Frederick. *Way's Packet Directory: 1848–1994.* Athens: Ohio University Press, 1994.

Winther, Oscar O. *The Transportation Frontier: Trans-Mississippi West, 1865–1890.* New York: Holt, Reinhart, and Winston, 1964.

# ILLUSTRATION CREDITS

Fig. 1.1. From John Luffman, *Geographic Principles* (London: Booth, 1803), map 1, courtesy Library of Congress, Geography and Map Division.

Fig. 1.2. From Seymor Dunbar, *A History of Travel in America* (New York: Tudor, 1937), 201.

Fig. 1.3. After Seymor Dunbar, *A History of Travel in America* (New York: Tudor, 1937), 39.

Fig. 1.4. From Seymor Dunbar, *A History of Travel in America* (New York: Tudor, 1937), 269.

Fig. 1.5. Courtesy Public Library of Cincinnati and Hamilton County.

Fig. 1.6. After T. C. Prudy, *Report on Steam Navigation in the United States* (Washington, D.C.: Department of the Interior, Census Office, 1880), 13–14.

Fig. 1.7. From the Captain Jim Howard Collection, courtesy Public Library of Cincinnati and Hamilton County.

Fig. 1.8. From the Captain Jim Howard Collection, courtesy Public Library of Cincinnati and Hamilton County.

Fig. 1.9. After T. C. Prudy, *Report on Steam Navigation in the United States* (Washington D.C.: Department of the Interior, Census Office, 1890).

Fig. 1.10. From the author's collection.

Fig. 1.11. From *Harper's Magazine,* 1858.

Fig. 2.1. From the author's collection.

Fig. 3.1. From Jean B. Marestier, *Memoir on Steamboats of the United States of America* (Paris: Royal, 1824), 77.

Fig. 3.2. After Alfred R. Maass, "Daniel French and the Western Steamboat Engine," *American Neptune* 56 (Winter 1996): 31.

Fig. 3.3. From James Renwick, *Treatise on the Steam Engine* (New York: Carvill, 1839), pl. V.

Fig. 3.4. Courtesy Library of Congress.

Fig. 3.5. Courtesy Special Collections, Tulane University Library.

Fig. 3.6. Courtesy American Philosophical Society.

Fig. 4.1. After Seymor Dunbar, *A History of Travel in America* (New York: Tudor, 1937), 381.

Fig. 4.2. From David Stevenson, *Sketch of the Civil Engineering of North America* (London: John Weale, 1838), 150.

Fig. 4.3. Courtesy Howard Steamboat Museum.

Fig. 4.4. By Kevin Crisman, Courtesy the Institute of Nautical Archaeology at Texas A&M University and the Oklahoma Historical Society.

Fig. 4.5. Courtesy Smithsonian American Art Museum.

Fig. 4.6. Courtesy Public Library of Cincinnati and Hamilton County.

Fig. 4.7. From Jean B. Maretier, *Memoir on Steamboats of the United States of America* (Paris: Royal, 1824), 80.

Fig. 4.8. From Jean B. Marestier, *Memoir on Steamboats of the United States of America* (Paris: Royal, 1824), 86.

Fig. 4.9. From Jean B. Marestier, *Memoir on Steamboats of the United States of America* (Paris: Royal, 1824), 81.

Fig. 4.10. After P. R. Hodge, *The Steam Engine, Its Origin and Gradual Improvement* (New York: D. Appleton, 1840), pl. XXII.

Fig. 4.11. After Alan L. Bates, *The Western Rivers Engineroom Cyclopoedium* (Louisville: Cyclopoedium, 1996), 17.

Fig. 4.12. From Norman S. Russell, "On American River Steamboats," *Transactions of the Insitution of Naval Architects* 2 (March 1855): 124.

Figs. 5.1. and 5.2. From Thomas Tredgold, *Machinery Used in Steam Navigation, Volume II, Part I* (London: John Weale, 1851), pls. 1 and 2.

Fig. 5.3. From Thomas Tredgold, *Machinery Used in Steam Navigation, Volume II, Part I* (London: John Weale, 1851), pl. 4.

Fig. 5.4. Courtesy Public Library of Cincinnati and Hamilton County.

Fig. 5.5. Courtesy Public Library of Cincinnati and Hamilton County.

Fig. 5.6. After Thomas Tredgold, *Machinery Used in Steam Navigation, Volume II, Part I* (London: John Weale, 1851), pl. 4.

Fig. 5.7. From Thomas Tredgold, *Machinery Used in Steam Navigation, Volume II, Part I* (London: John Weale, 1851), pl. 3.

Fig. 5.8. By Charles Fontayne and William S. Porter, courtesy Public Library of Cincinnati and Hamilton County.

Fig. 5.9. After Henry Hall, *Report on the Ship-Building Industry of the United States* (New York: Library Editions, 1970), 192.

Fig. 5.10. After Henry Hall, *Report on the Ship-Building Industry of the United States* (New York: Library Editions, 1970), 193.

Fig. 5.11. After Norman S. Russell, "On American River Steamers," *Transactions of the Institution of Naval Architects* 2 (1861): pl. XIV.

Fig. 5.12. Courtesy Alan Saltus, from Leslie C. Stewart-Abernathy (ed.), *Ghost Boats on the Mississippi* (Fayetteville: Arkansas Archaeological Survey, 2000), 73.

Fig. 5.13. From the author's collection.

Fig. 5.14. From the author's collection.

Fig. 5.15. From the author's collection.

Fig. 5.16. Courtesy R. Christopher Goodwin & Associates, Inc.

Fig. 5.17. After C. B. Kloppe, Andrew W. Hall, and Joe J. Simmons, *The A. S. Ruthven* (Austin: Southwest Underwater Archaeological Society and Texas Historical Commission, 1998), 31.

Fig. 5.18. Courtesy R. Christopher Goodwin & Associates, Inc.

Fig. 5.19. Courtesy R. Christopher Goodwin & Associates, Inc.

Fig. 5.20. After Norman S. Russell, "On American River Steamers," *Transactions of the Institution of Naval Architects* 2 (1861): pl. XIII.

Fig. 5.21. After C. B. Kloppe, Andrew W. Hall, and Joe J. Simmons, *The* A. S. Ruthven (Austin: Southwest Underwater Archaeological Society and Texas Historical Commission, 1998), 36.

Fig. 5.22. Courtesy R. Christopher Goodwin & Associates, Inc.

Fig. 5.23. After Charles Ward, "Shallow-Draught River Steamers," *Transactions of the Society of Naval Architects and Marine Engineers* 17 (1909): pl. 50.

Fig. 5.24. After Charles Ward, "Shallow-Draught River Steamers," *Transactions of the Society of Naval Architects and Marine Engineers* 17 (1909): pl. 38.

Fig. 5.25. From Thomas Tredgold, *Machinery Used in Steam Navigation, Volume II, Part I* (London: John Weale, 1851), pl. 5.

Fig. 5.26. From Charles Ward, "Shallow-Draught River Steamers," *Transactions of the Society of Naval Architects and Marine Engineers* 17 (1909): pl. 48.

Fig. 5.27. From Norman S. Russell, "On American River Steamers," *Transactions of the Institution of Naval Architects* 2 (1861): 124.

Fig. 5.28. After Allen R. Saltus, George J. Castille, and Charles E. Pearson, *Natchez under the Hill* (Baton Rouge: Coastal Environments, 1995), 323.

Fig. 5.29. After David L. Hedrick, *The Investigation of the Caney Creek Shipwreck Archaeological Site 41MG32* (College Station: Texas A&M University, 1998), 73.

Fig. 5.30. After David L. Hedrick, *The Investigation of the Caney Creek Shipwreck Archaeological Site 41MG32* (College Station: Texas A&M University, 1998), 71.

# INDEX

Page numbers in **bold** type refer to illustrations or figures.

paddle wheels (*cont.*)
hats, 124; construction of, 81–82, 86–87, 123–25; dimensions of, 82; flanges, 123, **124**; housings, 112, 123; placement of, 47–48, **47,** 50–51, 54, 82, 84–87; advantages over propellers, 81–82; shaft, 119–23, **123**
Palestine, Texas, 39
Panamerican Consultants, 36, 38
pantry, 92
*Paragon,* 45, **46,** 57
Parkersburg, Virginia, 39
pea, 78
Pearl River, 42
Pearson, Charles, 42
*Perseverance,* 57
Philadelphia, Pennsylvania, 21, 51
pig iron, exportation from the West, 15
pillow block, 123, **124**
pilot house, 90, 93
pine, *see* white pine *or* yellow pine
pirogues, 7
piston rod, 122
piston, 120–22
pitman, 122–23
Pittsburgh, Pennsylvania, 6, 11–12, 14–15, 18–24, 41, 45, 50, 52, 60, 62, **85**
planking: 107–108, 111; sacrificial, 107; use of sheet iron, 107
planters, *see* snags
poplar, use in steamboat construction, 97
poppet-valve system, 120–21
population of the East, 3
population of the West, 3, 11–12, 14, 17–18
pork, exportation from the West, 15
Porter, P.B., 11
Portsmouth, Ohio, 21, 39–40

*Post Boy,* 57
propellers, disadvantages of on the western rivers, 81–82
*Providence,* 57

Quartermaster Department, 40

R. Christopher Goodwin and Associates, *see* Goodwin and Associates
*R.J. Lackland,* 37
railroads, 15, 17–18
*Rapide,* 57
Red River, **25,** 25, 36
Red River Wreck, 34, 39–40, **35,** 63–64, **64**
*Reindeer,* 66
republic, Jeffersonian concept of, 4
rice production, 17
*Rifleman,* 57
Ringwalt, J.L., 19
Ripley, Ohio, 20
river cutoff, 27
river improvements, 8
river meander, 27, **28,** 30–31, 33, 128
River Salvage, 37
roads, 5–7, 127–28
*Robert Fulton,* 68–69, **68**
rocker arm, 121
*Rocket,* 57
Rock Island Rapids, 29
rock shaft, 121
Rocky Mountains, 6, 31
Roosevelt, Nicolas, 45
root knees, 102
rounded knuckle construction, 101, 103, **104**
rudder, 90, 105
Russell, Norman, 70, 103

safety valve, 48, 76–78, **78**
*Saint Louis,* 57